DADDY'S OXYGEN

TRIBUTE OF A DAUGHTER'S HEART: PAIN AND LEARNING THROUGH THE COVID-19 LOSS

SWAPNIL GAUR

I am writing this book in loving memory of my father as a tribute
to his enduring legacy and his profound impact on my life.

Dad's First Lesson: The ABCs of Life

"Daddy, you will forever be my hero, and your lessons will forever
be etched in my heart."

Contents

Introduction

These fourteen days were the most nerve-wracking and challenging days of my life. Each day, I watched my dad with a mixture of hope and prayer, desperately wishing for his recovery. Despite the dread and fickleness, those days have shaped me profoundly. Through my dad's wisdom and teachings, I learned to make better decisions and see life differently. His bravery and resilience became my guide, and I emerged from this experience with a deeper understanding of life's true essence.

In the wake of the global pandemic, the pain of losing a loved one to COVID-19 is a sorrow many share. This grief is a mix of sorrow, anger, love, and longing. It is a personal and shared experience, showing the sturdiness of the human spirit in the face of unprecedented challenges.

This journey through grief is marked by pain and sorrow but also by moments of unexpected grace and insight. It teaches us about our perseverance and our hearts' capacity to endure and heal. Through the pain, we honor the memories of those we have lost, carry their legacies forward, and find meaning amidst our sorrow.

This book is my way of navigating this journey, making sense of the pain, and finding a way forward. Through these pages, I hope to share my story, give voice to my grief, and honor the memory of a remarkable man who continues to light my path even in his absence.

Longing for Home

Living in Germany was an experience that felt worlds apart from my life in India. The rhythm of life was different; the days were often colder in more ways than one. Here, the warmth of a close-knit family was missing. There are no parents to wake me up with a gentle nudge, no one to fuss over me or push me to do things I sometimes resisted. In Germany, I learned the value of self-dependence and the importance of owning my life. I embraced new experiences in my career in the software industry, exploring Europe and my journey. Yet, despite the growth and independence, there was a persistent, aching void.

In the juggle of my life, I often traveled back to India to reconnect with my family, friends, and culture. Those trips were my lifeline, the thread that kept me connected to my roots. However, the previous year and this year had been particularly challenging. The COVID-19 pandemic has ravaged the world, and India has been hit hard. The virus spread like wildfire, and lockdowns became the new norm. Everything came to a standstill.

The dread for my family's safety in India consumed my thoughts. Despite daily video chats and constant updates, I missed the physical presence of my loved ones. I longed for the comfort of being with them, of sharing meals and laughter in person. The ambiguity was unbearable. In November 2021, as the world slowly began to recover and restrictions eased, I decided. It was time to go home.

I eagerly booked my flight tickets for the end of the year. Traveling during Christmas vacation was always expensive, and this year was no different. The prices were higher than usual, reflecting the pent-up demand from people who, like me, were eager to reunite with their families. I managed to secure a ticket with a return flight scheduled for February.

The anticipation of returning to India filled me with a mixture of excitement and nervousness. I couldn't wait to be surrounded by the familiar sounds and smells of India and to feel the embrace of my family. At the same time, I was aware of the fragility of the situation. The pandemic had taught me that nothing could be taken for granted.

As the days drew closer to my departure, I found myself reflecting on the contrasts between my life in Germany and India. Both worlds had shaped me in different ways, and I was grateful for the lessons each had taught me.

It was December 23, and the alarm rang to remind me it was time to start packing and shopping for my trip home. In just three days, I would be on a flight back to India, and with vacation started, I had more than a week off to enjoy until the New Year. The prospect of reuniting with my family brought a sense of excitement and anticipation that I hadn't felt in a long time.

As I ventured out to the shopping complex, my mind buzzed with thoughts of gifts I wanted to bring back for my family. I decided to video call my mom to get her input on what to buy. The call connected, and my dad picked up. "Where are you?" he asked, a hint of curiosity in his voice.

"I'm at the shopping complex," I replied. "Where's mom? I need to show her something."

"She's busy with her society friends and left her phone at home, as usual," he said with a chuckle. We both laughed, sharing a moment of light-hearted banter about her habit of forgetting her phone despite our constant reminders.

"So, what are you shopping for?" he inquired.

"Just jackets and some clothes," I said.

He couldn't resist. "What are you bringing for me?"

I smiled, knowing exactly what he meant. "I'll get you some nice Perfume," I assured him, aware of his passion for fragrances.

"Make sure you do," he emphasized, his excitement palpable even over the phone.

"Yes, I will," I repeated, just as my mom walked in. My dad, seizing the opportunity, started playfully scolding her for leaving her phone at home again.

"I wasn't expecting a call," she said, sitting down and laughing.

Dad handed the phone to her, and she eagerly started choosing jackets via the video call. These small, seemingly mundane moments were what I lived for—the simple, everyday interactions that connected us despite the miles between us.

After finalizing the choices with my mom, I hung up the call and continued shopping, my heart lighter from the joyful exchange.

Later, as I started packing, I thought about the significance of this trip. Packing for this trip was more than just organizing clothes and gifts; it was a process filled with emotions and reflections. Each item I packed was a symbol of my love and connection to my family. The jacket for my mom, a gift for my dad, and other little gifts for my family and friends—each represented a piece of my heart that I was bringing back home.

As I folded clothes and carefully placed the gifts in my suitcase, I imagined the hugs, the laughter, the shared meals, and the stories we would tell. The thought of my mom's cooking and my dad's stories filled me with a warmth that no amount of German efficiency could replace.

Soon, my dad's upcoming birthday on January 19 crossed my mind. He had a special fondness for electronic gadgets, so I decided to get some good gifts for him. Knowing my layover would be in Dubai, I planned to pick up something special for him there. I could already imagine his childlike excitement, as he always got excited about the gifts I brought from my travels.

Taking a break from shopping and packing, I sat down to relax while having coffee. A WhatsApp notification from my dad popped up, sharing random Facebook ad links of some Chinese electronic gadgets and smartwatches. I couldn't suppress a chuckle. I texted back, "What should I do with this?" He replied instantly, asking me to bring those if I find them in Germany, including remote selfie sticks and car mobile holders. I responded with a laughing emoji, knowing the chances were slim. He sent back a sad emoji, understanding my sarcasm. His tech enthusiasm and childlike curiosity always brought a smile to my face.

The next day, I planned a little Christmas celebration in town. While shopping, I found a stable Bluetooth selfie stick, which I knew would make dad happy. As I continued, I received a FaceTime call from dad. He was laughing and doing funny mimicry with animal filters, making me laugh out loud even amid stressful preparations. His love for technology and his ability to find joy in small things were infectious.

"Look at this!" he said, switching filters and making funny faces.

Later, my mom joined in, and soon the three of us were laughing together. These moments of lightheartedness were a precious reminder of the bond we share.

After a while, he asked, "Have you shared your flight details?"

"I'll share them with you. Dad," I replied.

As the sun began to set on December 25, I found myself nestled in the warmth of holiday celebrations, surrounded by friends and the festive spirit. The lights twinkled brightly, casting a cozy glow, but in the back of my mind, I was still creating a checklist of packing items I might forget, as well as reviewing regulation checks, including RT-PCR test results and vaccination certificate, before flying.

Resting after the day's celebrations, I received a call from my dad. His voice, filled with concern, brought me back to reality. "The news here is talking about the rising cases of the third wave of COVID," he said. "It's all over the news again. But I think it's not as severe now; it has become milder. But you still need to be careful and take all the necessary precautions."

"Yes, dad." There was a little unease and doubt in my voice.

He reminded me again, a bit louder this time, "When are you going to share your flight details?"

Laughing, I replied, "Yes, dad, now. I promise."

In the background, I could hear my mom's voice teasing him. "Give him your flight details already! You know he'll stay up all night tracking your flight and will do live commentary."

We all laughed together at her remark. "You don't have to keep tracking it all night, dad. Just check it once, and then it's okay."

"No, I have a habit of checking it," he insisted. "I feel excited about it."

His excitement was contagious, and it warmed my heart to know how much he cared. Our conversation continued, filled with light-hearted banter and shared laughter. Even through the phone, I could feel the love and connection.

Journey Home

The next day, December 26, arrived with a mix of emotions. I was excited to be heading home but also felt a pang of nervousness about the journey and the ongoing pandemic. I spent the day double-checking my packing, ensuring I had everything I needed.

As the evening approached, I said my goodbyes to my friends and headed to the airport. The Christmas lights and decorations seemed to bid me farewell, adding a touch of magic to my departure. My heart swelled with anticipation as I boarded the plane, knowing that in a few hours, I would be reunited with my People.

It was 1:00 AM UAE time when my flight landed in Dubai. Despite the late hour, the city was bustling, living up to its reputation as a global hub. I quickly connected to the airport Wi-Fi, eager to check messages and update my family. Almost immediately, my phone rang. It was my dad, calling from India where it was 2:30 AM. I wondered why he was still awake.

As I picked up, his voice burst through the speaker, sharp and full of energy. "Oh, you've reached!" he exclaimed, sounding as fresh as if it were the middle of the day.

"Dad, why are you still awake? You should be sleeping. You have to pick me up tomorrow," I said, my voice a mix of concern and amusement.

"Do you know that your connecting flight gate has changed, and it's been delayed by two hours?" he asked triumphantly as if he'd just revealed a secret.

I hadn't known. "No, I didn't know that yet."

"Now you know why I was tracking your flight," he replied with a chuckle.

I laughed, appreciating his diligence. "Okay, dad."

In the excitement of the moment, I blurted out, "I found something special for you here."

His voice lit up with curiosity. "Show me!"

I tried to show him through a video call, but the Wi-Fi connection was spotty. Despite the connection issues, he could sense my excitement. "Thanks for the flight information, Dad. I'll see you tomorrow morning. Have a good sleep."

"Yes, take care," he said, giving me the new gate and flight timing. His thoroughness made me feel at ease.

In the excitement of the moment, I blurted out, "I found something special for you here."

His voice lit up with curiosity. "Show me!"

I tried to show him through a video call, but the Wi-Fi connection was spotty. Despite the connection issues, he sensed my excitement. "Thanks for the flight information, Dad. I'll see you tomorrow morning. Have a good sleep."

"Yes, take care," he said, before giving me detailed information about the new gate and flight timing. His thoroughness made me feel at ease.

With a bit of time on my hands due to the delay, I roamed around the duty-free shops. I picked up a few surprises for his upcoming birthday. Despite the early hours, the airport was alive with travelers, and the shops were filled with many appealing items.

After spending some time navigating immigration and security, I finally made my way to the gate. The flight from Dubai to India was just a little over three and a half hours. As the plane took off, I felt a surge of excitement. The city lights of Dubai twinkled below, gradually fading into the darkness of the Arabian Sea. I leaned back in my seat, trying to catch some rest but finding it difficult with thoughts of home swirling in my mind.

Landing back in India after a long time in Europe felt incredibly comforting and familiar. The sights, sounds, and smells immediately brought back memories and a sense of belonging. As I went through customs and collected my luggage, my heart raced with excitement. Seeing the busy airport and hearing people speaking in my native language made me feel at home. The warmth and energy of the place filled me with joy and anticipation for the reunion with my family. It was like a homecoming. I knew my dad would be outside, waiting with the same excitement I felt.

As I walked out into the arrivals area, I spotted my parents immediately. My dad's face lit up when he saw me, and I rushed over, dropping my bags to embrace him. Everything seemed magical with my mom's warm hug.

"Welcome home!" he said, his voice thick with emotion.

"Thanks, dad," I replied, holding him tightly.

As we drove home, mom filled me in on all that had happened while I was away. Her voice was full of love and excitement, and dad was teasing us with our gossip; his voice was animated and full of life.

When we finally arrived home, the door opened to a chorus of excited greetings and warm hugs. My cousins and all the family members were there, their faces beaming with joy. The reunion was filled with laughter, stories, and a sense of togetherness that I had missed deeply. As we settled in for the night, the joy of being home filled my heart, promising a holiday season filled with love, laughter, and cherished memories. We enjoyed a lively family function and visited friends and family in different towns, soaking in the warmth and happiness of the season.

It was January 7 when my mom developed a fever. Despite taking numerous medicines, she didn't seem to feel any better. Doctor visits provided some relief, but her condition lingered. We dismissed it as a normal viral infection, with my dad noting that her weak immune system and diabetes slowed her recovery. We shared stories and cherished moments, hoping she would bounce back soon. By the next day, she started to feel a bit better. Everyone at home is excited about the marriage function in February. Preparations and shopping were in full swing, although I had to fly back to Germany before the event.

On January 12, my trip was planned for a week away from home, intending to return by the 19th and celebrate my dad's birthday with the whole family. On the evening of January 11, I argued with my dad about a financial decision I had made. He wasn't in favor of it, and despite my attempts to explain, he remained unconvinced. Our disagreements were typical, almost like siblings bickering, but this time, it felt different, more intense. We went to bed without resolving the issue, and the tension lingered.

The next morning, as I prepared to leave, I heard my dad mentioning about his cold and restless sleep last night. It didn't seem serious, so I didn't pay much attention. My goodbye to him was formal, tinged with a bit of ego from our unresolved argument. I hugged my mom warmly, savoring the magical comfort of her embrace, and left town.

While on vacation, I received a call from my dad three days later. He didn't ask how I was; instead, he immediately asked me to help one of his friend's children with a job referral. I understand his desire to help others instantly, and I respect him for it. Still carrying the frustration from our disagreement, I reluctantly agreed to help, and the conversation ended there. January 18, as I prepared to resume my home office after a long vacation, I struggled to connect to the VPN due to network issues.

I was anxious about starting work and frustrated with the situation. Although I was supposed to go home tomorrow, I now felt I should leave today. With this in mind, I called my mom. My voice was weak, but I managed to explain, "I couldn't connect to the VPN here, so I need to come home today. Can dad send someone to pick me up?"

She replied, her tone slightly anxious, "He's not well either. He has had a fever and cold for the last few days. When he takes medicine, it gets better for a while, but then it comes back."

Concerned, I asked, "Why didn't he call me? I know we had an argument, but he usually checks in."

"He's dull and weak," she said softly. "He's probably just tired."

Understanding the situation, I hurriedly packed and managed to get home by late evening. As I entered, I was puzzled to see my dad's karaoke with my cousin, appearing lively and normal. The sight was a jarring contrast to what I had imagined. I decided to stay silent and focus on my office work.

At dinner, my dad brought up my return plans. "Have you decided about your return on February 10? It's clashing with the family function."

His question, though innocent, added to my growing frustration. "You can go. I'll see what I will do," I snapped, trying to keep my irritation in check.

He tried to explain, "I'm just asking and trying to discuss."

Exhausted, I responded, "I haven't thought about anything yet, but I will let you know."

That night, an unspoken tension hung in the air. No one was in good health, and there was a tangible sense of agitation. We all went to bed without much conversation, each of us wrapped in our thoughts and worries.

Transitions in Life's Rhythm

The next morning, I woke to the sound of coughing. At first, I thought it was part of a dream, but the persistent, dry cough soon pulled me fully awake. My body was still tired from the previous days, but concern for my dad pushed me out of bed. I rushed to his room and found him sitting up, coughing uncontrollably.

"Dad, how are you feeling?" I asked, worry etched in my voice.

"I don't know," he replied between coughs. "I was fine till evening, but this morning, I can't stop coughing. It's making me restless."

Today was his birthday, a day I had planned to start with joy and celebration. But all thoughts of wishing him a happy birthday evaporated as I focused on his distress. The sound of his cough was eerily familiar, similar to the severe pollen allergies I sometimes experience. I quickly made him a cup of green herbal tea, hoping it would help as it usually did for me.

"Here, drink this. It should help with the cough," I said, handing him the steaming cup.

He took the tea and sipped it slowly, trying to calm his breathing. "Thank you," he said after a few moments. "I feel a bit better now."

But the relief was temporary. "I'm getting restless with this cough. I don't know what's happening all of a sudden."

I tried to encourage him. "Don't worry, dad. You'll be fine. Have you done an RT-PCR test?"

He shook his head. "No, it's just a viral infection. I didn't think it was necessary."

I insisted, "You need to get tested. It could be different for everyone. Let's not take any chances."

Reluctantly, he agreed. I immediately called a lab to arrange for an RT-PCR test at home. While we were waiting, his coughing intensified. "Call uncle. I might need to go to the hospital," he said, his voice strained.

Understanding the seriousness of the situation, I called my uncle, who arrived promptly. We all sensed that this could be more than just a viral infection. After a while, my mom brought the oxygen meter and tested his levels. The reading was 85, significantly lower than normal. Our doubts grew stronger, and we anxiously awaited the test results.

By this time, it was already afternoon. We were trying to arrange for a doctor's consultation, but first, we needed to admit him. This was not a good sign. While we were working on this, my mom asked my dad to eat something. He instantly refused.

I sat down beside my dad and softly said, "Happy Birthday." He replied with a quiet thank you, his voice low and lacking the usual birthday excitement.

To lighten the mood, I handed him the perfume I had bought for him, hoping to see a spark of joy. My dad usually celebrated even the smallest things in life, but today, he seemed very subdued. He only asked where I had bought it from. Trying to make him smile, I said, "Smell it, and if you can, you're safe from COVID, as people say." He smelled it and said, "Yes, I can smell it. It's a very nice fragrance." I joked, "Then you're safe from COVID." We all laughed a bit, easing the tension.

Just then, my uncle arrived and said to my dad, "Okay, get ready. We're going to admit you." The situation still didn't feel too intense or serious. Dad said, "Get my clothes. I'm going to get ready. Give me a water bottle and my mobile." I watched as he dressed up for the hospital, combing his hair and applying the perfume I had given him. We all believed that after a doctor's consultation and check-up, he would come home.

He told mom that she could come later and that they would see what the doctor said, and then they would both come home in the evening. My mom agreed. While he was getting ready to leave, mom packed a small bag of fruits for him in case he felt like eating later. We saw off my dad, who left with my uncle.

A little while later, my uncle called my mom. He told her to come to the hospital because they needed to take dad for a CT scan. They suspected it could be COVID. The RT-PCR report would take 48 hours to come back, so even if it was COVID, it might not be as serious as we feared. But now, our initial calm was turning into concern. The situation is becoming a bit more serious.

An hour after my mom left, a wave of apprehension began to sweep over me. Alone in the house, everything felt eerily quiet, and a sense of dread started creeping in. My mind raced with worry about my dad, and my body seemed to react to this tension, my heartbeat syncing with my rising apprehension. I grabbed my phone and called my mom, my voice trembling, "Where are you, mom? Is dad okay?"

She answered, her voice a mix of concern and calm, "We're at the laboratory for the CT scan. They think he has COVID, but we'll know for sure with the CT report tomorrow. The doctors have told us to take all necessary precautions. We need to wear proper masks and use PPE kits, and we can't be in the same room with him for now. We'll have to decide tomorrow because if it's confirmed, we'll need to admit him to a COVID hospital."

The gravity of the situation was sinking in, and I felt a wave of restlessness. My concerns were no longer abstract; they were becoming reality. Unable to stay home any longer, I decided to go to the hospital to see my dad and bring him some food.

When I arrived at the hospital, I found my dad in his room. He was sitting there, looking more like himself, without a mask. Now and then, though, I noticed him putting the mask on, taking deep breaths of oxygen whenever he felt restless. Despite the tension in the air, he seemed to be managing as best as he could.

I approached him, trying to keep my voice steady, "dad, how are you feeling?"

He gave a faint smile, "I'm alright, just a little tired. They're running all these tests, but most of the time I feel fine. It's only when I get breathless that I need the extra o2."

Seeing him like this, maintaining a semblance of normalcy despite everything, tugged at my heart. I handed him the food I had brought, hoping to provide some comfort. "I brought you something to eat. You need to keep your strength up."

He took the food, and his smile was a bit stronger this time. "Thank you. It's good to see you. Don't worry too much, okay? We'll get through this."

His words were reinforcement, but the skepticism of the situation loomed over us. As we sat together, thoughts of the days ahead occupied my mind, what they might bring. The future felt uncertain, and all we could do was take things one step at a time.

I sat in the hospital room, feeling a heavy weight on my heart. The doctors had instructed us to take strict precautions around dad, to treat him as if he wasn't the same person we knew, to stay distant, to avoid close contact. This was a stark and painful shift from our usual interactions. The pandemic had forced us to behave unnaturally, and the emotional toll was immense. It was heartbreaking to keep my distance from dad, to not be able to sit beside him and talk his heart out.

This sudden change was a harsh reminder of how the pandemic impacted people, not just physically but psychologically. It altered the way we connected with our loved ones, injecting worry and caution into every interaction. It was as if an invisible wall had been erected between us, making the already difficult situation even harder to bear.

As the day went on, more friends and family members learned about dad's condition. They reached out over the phone, anxious for updates. Their voices were filled with concern and support, but few could visit due to the hospital's strict regulations. People themselves were hesitant to come, aware of the risks and wanting to keep everyone safe.

The constant stream of calls and messages was overwhelming. Each conversation was a reminder of how serious the situation was, and how much support we had. It was a strange mix of feeling isolated yet surrounded by concern.

Despite the precautionary measures and the physical distance, I tried to engage with dad as much as I could. I asked him about his day, and how he was feeling, and shared little stories to keep his spirits up. He appreciated the effort, though I could see the little sadness in his eyes, the same sadness I felt in my heart.

The room was filled with an unsettling quiet, interrupted only by the beeping of medical equipment and occasional footsteps in the hallway. I found myself lost in thought, reflecting on how drastically life has changed in such a short time. The apprehension of the unknown, the need for caution, and the emotional distance from loved ones were all new realities we had to accept.

Hours passed, and the weight of the situation became heavier. I looked at dad, who was trying to rest, his breathing sometimes aided by the oxygen mask. The pandemic had turned our world upside down, but amidst the distress and dilemma, there was a glimmer of hope. We were all doing our best to navigate this new reality, holding onto the belief that things would eventually get better.

It was already night, and as the hours crept by, the sense of anxiety deepened. My mother is still recovering from a fever, which we suspected was COVID-19. Despite this, she insisted on staying at the hospital with my dad. I was worried about her health, but she and my dad both insisted I go home. They assured me that the house wasn't far, and my mom wanted to stay with dad. Reluctantly, I agreed, knowing this night would be a long one as we awaited the results the next morning.

The mere mention of the hospital made everything feel more intense, and it created a cloud of worry in my mind. I said goodnight to my parents and uncle and left, promising dad that we would celebrate his birthday when he came home. Dad agreed and laughed softly, saying, "Yes, we will celebrate together."

As I reached home late on that winter night, the reality hit me hard. I had never felt so scared in my own house. Every shadow seemed to haunt me, and the silence was oppressive. I struggled to hold back my tears, praying fervently for my parents' health. They were my family, my friends, my biggest supporters, and seeing them weak is unbearable.

I sat on my bed, feeling the weight of the night pressing down on me. It was 11:30 PM, and the silence was so profound that I could hear my breath. I knew this night would be etched in my memory forever as everything seemed to be turning upside down. I hadn't eaten dinner; I didn't have an appetite, consumed by worry. I called my mom every twenty minutes, anxious about dad's oxygen levels and overall condition. She maintained her patience, providing updates despite my frequent calls. Dad hadn't slept either, undoubtedly worried, though he upheld the strong pillar he had always been.

On one of the calls, he allayed our fears, "Please don't worry. Sleep peacefully. Whatever happens, we'll face it tomorrow. I'm fine now. I don't have any issues." His calm voice provided some comfort, but the worry gnawed at me.

I told my mom, "mom, we'll bring dad home. Hospitals can be draining, and the intensity there is overwhelming. Even if he has COVID, we'll take care of him at home, and he will be fine." She agreed, sharing my concerns about the hospital's atmosphere.

It was 3:30 AM by then. My mom, her voice filled with love, told me, "Don't worry too much now. Sleep, child. We are fine, and everyone here is ready to help."

I decided it was time to let them rest, too. I wished them a final goodnight and tried to settle into sleep, hoping that the morning would bring better news. The night was filled with silence, but knowing my parents were there, facing this together, gave me a sliver of peace. This was a night that would stay with me forever, marking a moment when life's fragility became all too real.

A Tale of 14 days

DAY One: A Heavy Heart and Determined Spirit

Wide awake at 4:00 AM, my mind racing with thoughts and worries, still echoing my mom's words of comfort from an hour ago. The silence of the house felt oppressive, intensifying my worry.

I tried to resist the urge to call her again. I knew they needed rest, and I didn't want to disturb them unnecessarily. But as the minutes ticked by, my unease grew stronger, and the need to hear my mom's voice became overpowering. I couldn't hold back any longer.

Grabbing my phone with trembling hands, I dialed her number. Each ring seemed to stretch out endlessly until she finally answered. Her voice, though tired, was filled with the warmth I needed to hear.

"Mom, how's dad? How are you?" I asked, my voice barely concealing the panic I felt.

"He's resting; the doctors are keeping a close watch on him. I'm fine too, just a bit tired," she replied, trying to sound calm and composed.

"What about his oxygen level?" I pressed, desperate for any information.

As mom spoke with me, she quietly approached dad's bed, which was some distance away, noting she hadn't checked on him for a while as he slept. But now, she noticed something different in the sound of his breathing. It wasn't his usual snoring.

"Could you check his oxygen level?" I asked, worry knotting my chest.

"Yes, he's sleeping without the oxygen mask. I'll go and check on him," she replied. I made sure to remind her to wear a mask before going into his room, and she agreed.

While still on the call, she approached dad's bed and placed the oximeter on his finger. The reading was seventy-seven. Her voice trembled as she said, "It's so low."

My heart skipped a beat. "Check it again," I urged, hoping it was a mistake. She did, but the reading was still alarmingly low at 78.

We were both scared. Mom moved quickly, placing the mask over his face. Dad rested in a deep sleep, seemingly unaware of the flurry of activity around him.

For a moment, there was silence on the call, a heavy, intimidated silence. Then, trying to comfort both of us, I said, "Don't worry. Everything will be fine. Trust in God. We have good medical treatments now, better processes, and effective medicines. Everything will be okay in the end. Let's wait for the CT scan and RT-PCR results tomorrow."

I assured her that I would come to the hospital in the morning and uncle would be there too. "Don't worry, and take care of yourself," I urged her. "Can you check his oxygen level again?"

She did, and this time, the reading was much better, at ninety-three and climbing to ninety-eight. It was a relief to see the numbers improve. "Dad is resting properly now," she said, her voice calmer.

"Get some sleep, mom. I'm sorry to have disturbed you, but I was extremely restless."

"It's okay," she replied softly. "Take care of yourself, and I'll see you in the morning. Bring some tea from home; I need my home tea. Dad would like it, too. The results should be ready by 9 AM."

"Okay, mom. Goodnight. See you in the morning."

"Goodnight. Take care," she said, and we hung up.

I lay back in bed, the tension in my body slowly easing. The night had been filled with moments of intense distress, but now, there was a sliver of hope. Dad's oxygen levels had stabilized, and mom was there with him. I closed my eyes, trying to find some rest, knowing that in a few hours, I would be back at the hospital, ready to face whatever came next.

I fell asleep, exhausted by the weight of the situation. Waking up around 6:15 AM, I felt restless and unsure about the day ahead. Not wanting to disturb my parents again, I took some time to myself, recognizing the need for calm and composure. With a cup of tea in hand, I took a deep breath and allowed myself a few moments of quiet reflection. Centering myself, I performed some breathing exercises and softly chanted, finding comfort in familiar routines.

After a refreshing bath, I surrendered my worries to the higher power, praying for my dad and my family. I sat in my small worship area for about 30 minutes, talking to the universe and seeking peace and guidance. This practice helped me feel more optimistic and at peace.

Venturing outside by 7:30 AM to catch the sunrise, I hoped for calm. Instead, I found a dense fog cloaking the silent streets, broken only by the occasional bark of a dog. The weather mirrored the intensity of our situation. Returning inside, I headed to the kitchen. I infused the tea with herbs and prepared it along with sandwiches for my mom and dad. Once everything was ready, I left for the hospital. Upon arriving at my dad's room, I found my mom sitting outside. Concern was etched on her face.

"What happened?" I asked gently.

She sighed, "I was worried about him and the test results. I didn't want to disturb you since you hadn't slept much."

I peered into the room and saw dad sleeping, his oxygen levels in the safe range. "It's okay, mom. You know dad is strong. He's fully vaccinated, and the current strain of COVID isn't as severe. People are recovering from it more easily now. Have faith."

She nodded, sharing stories of dad's endurance. She reminded me of his past setbacks: his appendix operation when he was young that led to a serious infection, his critical condition during that time, and his miraculous recovery. She recounted his open-heart surgery after three major heart attacks, a time when the doctors had been skeptical for eight days if he would survive. Yet, through it all, dad's strong belief and determination had pulled him through.

I took her hand, "He will come out of this, too. Trust in everything."

She seemed better after our conversation, and we sat outside, sipping tea. Uncle arrived with snacks and fruits, and we began discussing our next steps.

Uncle explained, "It depends on the infection's spread and its severity. This isn't a COVID-registered hospital, and they want us to transfer dad to one that has a COVID ward."

We agreed that waiting for the results is the only option. Mom suggested that I should go home since I was working remotely. Leaving uncle with mom, I took one last look at dad, who was sleeping peacefully and headed home.

The day was just beginning, and while suspicion loomed, we clung to hope and the belief that dad's strength would see him through once more. As I walked away from the hospital, I felt a mix of fear and faith, knowing that whatever comes, we have to fight it.

I had just returned from a long vacation and rejoined the office yesterday. Today, I found myself struggling to focus on work. My mind was consumed with worry, each tick of the clock syncing with my mounting fear as I waited for my dad's test results. At 10:30 AM, I called my uncle, but he said they were still waiting for the reports. He assured me that they would inform me as soon as the results came.

Trying to manage my responsibilities, I emailed my office to convey the seriousness of my situation. They were incredibly supportive, telling me to only handle urgent tasks and to prioritize my family. Grateful for their understanding, I took the day off to be with my loved ones.

At around 11:00 AM, my phone rang. It was my uncle. "We're shifting dad to a new hospital. His results are in. He has a COVID infection," he said.

My heart sank. "Can we bring him home? He would recover well at home," I asked, hoping for a simpler solution.

"No, we can't. His CT score is 20/25. It's critical," he replied.

I was unfamiliar with the significance of those numbers, but the word "critical" resonated loudly. "Which hospital?" I asked, trying to stay calm.

He gave me the name and asked me to come over. After hanging up, I quickly searched online to understand what a CT score of 20/25 means. The information I found was alarming, and my mind swirled with questions and apprehensions. How did he get this infection? Why is his condition so severe compared to others? What does this mean for his recovery?

By the time my cousins arrived at my house, I was already feeling overwhelmed. They came to offer support and discuss our next steps. They, too, were not in the best of health, showing symptoms of cough and light fever. The atmosphere was heavy with concern and ambivalence.

We sat together, trying to piece together how we had reached this point. Each of us voiced our worries, and the sense of helplessness was evident. Everything seemed to be turning negative, and the situation felt increasingly dire.

We decided to head to the hospital together. As I prepared to leave, I tried to steady myself, knowing that I needed to be strong for my family. We gathered our things, exchanged a few encouraging words, and set off to face whatever awaited us at the hospital. The journey there felt surreal, each passing moment filled with a mixture of dread and determination.

I was hesitant to call my mom at this moment. The nervousness of what I might hear gripped me tightly.

Instead, I reached the hospital around 1 PM, searching for my uncle's car or any sign of my mom and uncle. My cousins and I tried calling both, but neither answered, which heightened our worry. Desperate, I called my dad's number, hoping someone else might pick up.

To my surprise, it was dad who answered. "Hello," I heard his voice, which I hadn't expected.

"Dad, where are you? No one is picking up. How are you?" I asked, my voice tinged with relief and concern.

"I'm outside the hospital building. I'm fine. Your mom and uncle are inside the hospital handling the formalities," he replied.

"Can you guide me to where you are? We're coming over," I said.

He shared his live location, and I quickly made my way to him. When I reached, I saw him standing there, looking a bit weary but still smiling.

"Hello, dad. Are you okay?" I asked.

"Yes, I am, but I feel breathless after walking for a bit without the oxygen mask," he admitted.

"Of course, dad. You don't need to worry about any of this. You'll be fine. We're all here with you, and this will be over in a couple of days," I put him at ease.

He nodded, smiling faintly. "What exactly did my results say? Do you know?"

"You have a COVID infection, but you're fully vaccinated. You're strong, dad. It's nothing to worry about," I said, trying to keep my voice steady.

He smiled again, "Yes, everything will be fine."

Just then, my mom and uncle arrived and informed us that we needed to go inside. Dad, showing his usual stubborn bravery, jumped out of the ambulance and began walking toward the building without his oxygen mask. His courage and determination to handle things his way are evident, but as he walked a few steps, he became breathless. He was still trying to push through when we noticed him struggling.

"What are you doing?" we called out.

"I'm fine. I'm going inside on my own," he insisted.

"No, you can't do that," we replied, concerned.

An attendant quickly came over, guided dad to a chair, and helped him put on his mask. As he sat down, his breathlessness turned to panic, realizing the severity of his condition. We watched, hearts heavy, as he rushed to the ICU ward.

In our protective PPE kits, we followed cautiously, but the hospital staff asked us to stay away, which was incredibly tough. It was hard to leave dad alone in such a critical condition. After some requests, they allowed only two of us to accompany him. My uncle and I decided to go inside.

Reaching dad's bed, we found him still struggling with his breathing, his oxygen levels perilously low at seventy-five. The doctors instructed him to relax and emphasized that he couldn't walk around anymore; he had to accept the reality of his health condition. He nodded, understanding, and lay back to rest.

"We're here to support you, dad," I said softly, holding his hand. "You need to rest and let us take care of everything."

He looked at us with a mix of gratitude and resignation. "Thank you. I know I'll be fine with you all here."

We stayed by his side, offering him the comfort of our presence, hoping our support would help him find the fortitude to fight through this challenging time.

After a while, dad's oxygen levels and other vitals stabilized. With his reports in hand, we saw that he was in a relatively stable condition, albeit weakened. I was relieved to see the confidence in his eyes, a trait that had always been his greatest asset. We encouraged him to rest, and he nodded, acknowledging his need for sleep.

Uncle and I approached the doctor to understand the full scope of dad's health situation. The doctor explained, "He has a critical level of infection, but it can be cured with intense care, appropriate medications, and close monitoring. We need to conduct additional tests to measure his blood oxygen levels and other parameters. For now, we've started treatment for COVID-19, but we'll need to wait for further results to determine the best course of action."

We agreed to the plan and were asked to leave the area to allow dad to rest. As we were leaving, I felt a strong urge to see dad once more. Peeking into his room, I saw him resting with his eyes closed. Sensing my presence, he opened his eyes and smiled weakly.

"You can go now," he said softly. "I feel good."

I glanced at the monitor and saw his vitals were stable. "Have you eaten anything today?" I asked.

He chuckled, "Yes, some sandwiches, fruit salad, and lots of medicines."

I laughed with him, relieved to see his sense of humor intact. "Don't worry. We've been asked to let you rest, and that's what you need most right now. We'll see you in the evening during visiting hours. Everything will be fine, I promise."

He looked at me with a mix of concern and reassurance. "Don't worry too much about me. Take care of yourselves. It seems like everyone has COVID symptoms. Make sure everyone gets an RT-PCR test, especially your mom. She must be really worried and isn't well herself."

"I will, dad. I'll make sure everyone gets tested and looked after," I assured him.

At that moment, the doctor entered the room and instructed dad to take steam inhalation three times a day and mentioned that he would need some additional therapies. We nodded in agreement.

As we left the room, i felt a mix of relief and trepidation. Dad was stable for now, but the road to recovery is still uncertain. His bravery and determination were evident, but the reality of his condition weighed heavily on us all.

Back home, the atmosphere was tense. My cousins, already showing symptoms of cough and light fever, listened intently as we relayed the doctor's update. We discussed the importance of getting tested and taking precautions to prevent the spread of the infection within the family.

By late afternoon, we had arranged for everyone to take RT-PCR tests. I made sure my mom, who was already not feeling well, got the necessary nurturing and encouragement.

Despite her illness, she is deeply worried about dad, her concern evident in every word she speaks.

As evening approached, we prepared to return to the hospital. My mind raced with thoughts and prayers for dad's swift recovery. I gathered some items he might need, including a fresh set of clothes and his favorite snacks, hoping to bring him some comfort.

A Fragile Encounter

The feeling of dread settled heavily in my chest as I approached the ICU ward. The very thought of seeing my dad in such a vulnerable state filled me with apprehension. Clad in a PPE kit, I couldn't shake off the unease that enveloped me as I made my way through the hospital floors. As I reached the ICU, I discovered that my father's bed had been moved. Suddenly, from across the room, he recognized me through my PPE kit. His eyes, though tired, lit up with recognition. "Naina!" he called out, using my nickname. He immediately sat up in bed, removed his mask, and smiled at me. Relieved, I hurried to his side. "What all things did you bring?" he asked, eyeing the large bag I carried.

With a humorous tone, I replied, "Everything you want is here." His laughter was a comforting sound in such environments. "Do you have something to eat?" he inquired. I handed him the evening tea, snacks, and his phone, which we had requested the doctor to allow. His joy was distinct.

"How are you feeling?" I asked, concern evident in my voice.

"I am fine," he assured me. "I've been taking steam and doing some breathing exercises, but mostly I feel like resting. I get bored sometimes; hospital life isn't tough, but it's monotonous. It's good that you brought my phone. How are things at home? Did you all get tested?"

"Yes, all of us did. Since I am fine, I haven't been tested. Someone has to come to the hospital for you," I replied.

He nodded thoughtfully, then added, "Don't bring mom here now. Her immunity is already low."

I agreed, understanding the gravity of the situation. Our conversation was interrupted by the doctor, who came to check on my dad. Dad, sitting without his mask, answered, "I am fine. Feeling much better now, though I do feel weak."

The doctor explained, "There's a heavy impact from the medications." I sat next to his bed when he asked, "Is my lung function at 20%, or is it 20% damaged? I got a CT score of twenty. What does this number mean?"

I explained, with the doctor nodding in agreement, "Neither. The score represents the extent of the infection in your lungs. Out of 25, 20 of your lung segments are infected, but it's recoverable."

The doctor smiled at our earnest discussion and advised, "Don't overthink it. Focus on the mandatory precautions and treatments. Continue with the breathing exercises, frequent steam inhalation, and physiotherapy. Do more of these than what we provide here; it will help your lungs regain strength."

We both agreed to follow his advice. The doctor handed me a list of medications and tests that needed to be done as our visit came to an end.

"Sit with me for ten more minutes," he requested softly.

As we continued our conversation, my dad requested that I bring the steam machine from home. He explained that it would be easier for him to take steam frequently if he had it. "Sure, I'll bring it tomorrow," I promised. From my bag, I took out a small idol of Lord Hanuman and placed it beside his bed. Seeing him, my dad bowed down reverently and said, "It's good that you brought him." His belief in Lord Hanuman was immense, providing him with both fortitude and peace of mind.

"From Him, you get all might, courage, and faith," I said softly. "He will listen to your prayers." My dad nodded, touching the idol's feet with deep devotion.

I didn't want to leave him, but I knew I had to. "Dad, I should go now," I said reluctantly. "Uncle will come to see you later this evening, and we will see each other tomorrow morning. Take care of yourself and have faith that everything will be fine. You look better already, and I feel that it won't be long before you're home celebrating your birthday."

With full confidence, he replied, "Take care of everyone at home and yourself." I placed my hand on his shoulder and soothe him, "Don't think you're alone in this journey. We are just one call away, and I am already missing you at home."

It was an emotional moment as I prepared to leave. I booked all the tests for dad at the hospital counter and bought the necessary medicines, which I handed to the doctor. As I left the hospital, heading home, the heavy winter fog outside seemed to mirror the fog of unpredictability within me. But I knew that facing and fighting the situation was all we could do; we had to prepare for whatever lay ahead.

Life is like a game where everyone is running, and one day, you might be left behind, slip, or get out of the game entirely. These thoughts weighed heavily on my mind as I walked through the cold, shivering not just from the weather but from the intense emotions within me. Tears welled up in my eyes, and I could no longer hold them back. I had woken up this morning praying that nothing serious would happen, unaware of how intense the situation would become.

The cold air bit at my face, but it was the ache in my heart that truly chilled me. Each step I took away from the hospital felt heavier with every stride, burdened with worry and the desperate hope that my dad would recover soon.

As I made my way home, I resolved to stay strong, to be the pillar my dad needed me to be. Life's unpredictability is daunting, but it was also a reminder of the rese we must summon in times of adversity. And so, with a heavy heart but a determined spirit, I continued forward, ready to face whatever comes next.

We ate dinner at home without speaking much to each other, each lost in our thoughts. I felt tired and overwhelmed with emotions and eventually fell asleep without even realizing it.

DAY Two: The Strength of Small Things

At the crack of dawn, precisely at 6:00 AM, the persistent ringing of a video call shattered the early morning silence, abruptly pulling me from my sleep. Confused and disoriented, I struggled to clear my head and locate my phone. A surge of panic coursed through me as I fumbled to answer, my heart racing with worry. To my immense relief and surprise, my dad's face appeared on the screen, his broad smile instantly soothing my frayed nerves. Despite his efforts to maintain a strong front, the twinkle in his eyes betrayed his true emotions. With characteristics of warmth and a touch of calmness, he asked if I could bring him a comforting cup of morning tea from home. This simple request filled me with a mix of tenderness and urgency to fulfill his morning wish.

"Sure, dad, I will be there in half an hour." "As the nurse came in to provide an update, he quickly ended the call."

Supporting my back, I stood up in bed and took several deep breaths to prepare for the day ahead. A mix of emotions churned within me—worry, determination, and a touch of hope. After a few moments of gathering myself, I made sure not to disturb anyone at home, especially my mom, who hadn't slept well the previous night. She had struggled to find rest (a common occurrence these days), and I didn't want to add to her worries. I splashed some cold water on my face, which woke me up completely and then headed to the kitchen. I wanted to prepare tea as well as possible, infusing it with herbs to provide extra comfort and healing. The tea brewed, I freshened up and dressed warmly for the winter morning, ensuring I had my PPE kit ready for the hospital visit. I poured the tea into a thermos, making a little extra, just in case.

Within 20 minutes, I was ready. Gently, I approached my mom's room and gently called, "Mom, I'm leaving for the hospital to meet dad." It took a few attempts to wake her, and she stirred with nervousness. "Why? What happened?" she asked, disoriented and worried.

"Don't worry, mom, everything is fine," I allayed her fears. "Dad video called a few minutes ago. He's okay; he just wants some tea from home."

She sighed with relief but insisted, "I will join you. Wait for a few minutes; I want to meet him."

I knew she wasn't well and strongly advised against her coming. "No, mom. You're not well, and it's better if you stay home. I'll video call you from the hospital so you can talk to dad. Please don't worry."

Though desperate to see him, she understood the consequences and reluctantly agreed to stay. Still, she got up immediately and asked me to wait for ten more minutes while she prepared a fruit salad and protein snacks for dad. I couldn't refuse her earnest request.

With the herbal tea and the snacks my mom had lovingly prepared, I quickly remembered the steamer he had asked me to bring the day before, so I hurried to grab that as well. I felt a sense of mission as I headed to the hospital. These small tokens of comfort were more than just food and drink; they carried our love, hope, and support to my father, who needed every bit of resolve we could offer.

Walking through the quiet corridors of the hospital, my heartbeat quickened, syncing with the echoing sirens and the rhythmic hum of the vital monitors around. Each step heightened my anticipation. As I neared the ICU, the sterile surroundings seemed to press in, the weight of the moment heavy with the aura of visiting hours. A nurse's nod granted me entry.

Excitement and concern surged within me as I neared the threshold, unsure of what lay beyond the door. Yet, when I turned the handle, his gaze met mine as if he had been waiting for me. Words were unnecessary; our shared love and concern spoke volumes.

Seeing him and being near him filled me with immense joy. His smiling face was a comforting sight. As I poured his tea and served the snacks, I found myself bombarding him with questions. "How are you feeling? Were you able to sleep last night? What about your test results? Did the doctor come by?"

He sipped the tea and, with his characteristic calm, put my mind at ease, "I am perfectly okay. Don't panic. As long as I have my family, with you around me, I will get through everything." He went on to explain that the doctor had visited earlier that morning, checked on him, and said everything looked fine, although another RT-PCR test was needed. He mentioned that he had been slowly doing his breathing exercises, taking steam twice a day, and spending his time praying, reading, and listening to music. The doctor has noted that everything is fine in the reports, except for his oxygen levels, but he was optimistic about recovery.

As we sat there, he began sharing his life experiences, emphasizing the importance of strong family bonds. "I've faced challenges in health, job, and relationships before, but with a strong family, the biggest problems in life seem small. Family protects you from bad experiences and always provides the best solutions without any ill intentions." He paused, looking at me with deep affection. "Seeing you enter the door gives me courage," he said, his eyes shining with sincerity.

At that moment, I felt a profound connection with my father. His words resonated deeply within me, reminding me of the unbreakable bond we shared. His unwavering faith in the power of family, even in the face of illness, was both humbling and inspiring. His calm demeanor and positive outlook were infectious.

As soon as I handed steamer, which he demanded, he eagerly said, "Let me take the steam now and do some exercises while you're here." He set up the steamer and started his breathing exercises, using the device where he had to blow balls into the air, demonstrating his lung capacity and bravery.

With determination in his eyes, he remarked, "I will try to target these balls to its level." Watching him, I felt a swell of pride. His dedication and endurance were inspiring, and I felt compelled to praise and encourage him. "You're doing great, dad. Keep it up."

As he continued his exercises, a nurse entered the room. She noticed the steamer and curiously inquired about it. My dad, always charming and convincing, introduced me to the nurse and began to explain how this portable steamer worked. His enthusiasm was infectious. He demonstrated the process with such skill and confidence that the nurse seemed genuinely fascinated.

"Your dad is good at this," she said to me with a smile. "He's convinced me to the point that I want to get one of these for myself. Could you send me an online link to buy one?"

My dad's ability to engage and persuade, even in such a setting, was truly remarkable. Despite his condition, he maintained a spirit that could uplift those around him. The nurse's admiration was just another proof of his enduring determination and character.

As he finished his demonstration, he turned back to his exercises, his face set with determination. I watched him, feeling a mix of awe and deep affection. Here he is, in a hospital bed, yet he is still the same strong, resourceful, and charismatic man I had always known. His ability to adapt, to find fortitude in the small things, and to keep pushing forward is a lesson in determination.

As visiting time drew to a close, a nurse gently informed me that I needed to leave. Reluctantly, I turned to my dad, my heart heavy with the knowledge that I had to go. "Please take care of yourself, Dad," I requested, trying to keep my voice steady.

He smiled at me, that same comforting smile that always managed to uplift me. "I will, Naina. Don't worry. And remember to take care of your mom. She needs a positive environment now more than ever."

His words, filled with concern and love, echoed in my mind. He was always thinking of everyone, even in his own time of need. I promised him that I would take care of Mom, trying to infuse my voice with as much optimism and resolve as I could gather. "I'll see you this evening,

Dad. We'll get through this together."

As I slowly made my way out of the room, I felt a profound sense of sadness and turned back one last time to see him waving, his eyes filled with unwavering faith and determination.

As I exited the hospital, I couldn't shake the image of my dad's brave face from my mind. His love and positivity are a source of fortitude for me. I knew that our connection would carry us through, and I resolved to stay strong for both him and my mom.

I feel scared and restless because everyone in my family is sick and has a fever. During this pandemic, not many friends or family members can help. It feels like the psychological impact of the situation is breaking people more than the disease itself. There's a lack of help and support, and we have to keep our distance from loved ones. The trepidation of the disease spreading suddenly looms over us. Each day starts with the puzzle, and it feels like anything could happen with my next breath. The weight of this persistent worry is overwhelming, making it hard to find peace or hope.

As I was leaving for home, I reflected on the importance of staying positive during this crucial time and creating a supportive atmosphere for my mom. Her sensitivity and inner turmoil were obvious, and it was up to all of us to ensure she felt soothed and optimistic.

When I reached home, I learned that our house help had also refused to come due to fright of COVID-19. With mom still not fully recovered, we were now overwhelmed by the responsibilities. To alleviate some of the burden, my uncle offered to manage things at the hospital in the evening and visit dad while we handled things at home for the day.

At night, while my uncle and brother were at the hospital, we chatted with dad over a video call. "How are you getting on, dad?" we asked.

"I'm perfectly fine," he replied, showing us his stable oxygen levels on the monitor without wearing an oxygen mask.

We were all relieved to see this and felt hopeful that everything would be fine soon. Dad smiled and said, "Take care of each other, and don't ignore any COVID symptoms."

His words gave us confidence. Ending the call, we silently vowed to support each other and stay vigilant about our health, inspired by his perseverance and positivity.

DAY Three: Strength in the Face of Fear

By 8 AM, I was anxiously waiting for my dad's morning call. When it didn't come, dread settled in my chest. Repeated attempts to reach him were met with silence, which only intensified my consternation. My sense of dread grew, and I felt a strong need to get to the hospital quickly and see him myself.

While I prepared to leave for the hospital, my mom expressed her desire to accompany me. Having recovered from her health issues, she has been feeling somewhat better lately. I understood her strong desire to see dad, making it hard to deny her requests. Yet, I was also deeply concerned about her exposure to the hospital environment, especially given her recent illness.

"Mom," I said gently, "I understand you want to see dad, and I promise you'll get to see him this evening. Morning visits are short, and you need more rest. By evening, you'll feel even better, and you can have a longer visit with him."

She looked at me, her eyes filled with both determination and concern. "But I want to see him now," she insisted. "Even though you give updates after each visit, I want to see him myself to make sure he is okay."

I took a deep breath, trying to balance my turbulence with the need to steady her. "I know, mom. I do. But we must take major precautions. I'll arrange another PPE kit for you, and we'll make sure you're completely protected when you visit this evening."

Her face softened as she considered my words. After a moment, she nodded and quietly said, "Alright, but make sure to take care of yourself too."

I was overwhelmed with relief as she agreed to wait until the evening. "I'll take good care of myself. And I'll bring back any updates from the morning visit." I said, giving her a gentle, soothing grin.

She seemed convinced, and I could see the tension in her shoulders ease slightly. "Okay," she repeated, her voice steadier now.

"He'll be so happy to know you're coming," I assured her.

As I left the house, I felt a mixture of emotions. I was relieved that mom had agreed to rest and take precautions, but I also felt the weight of responsibility for both her and dad. The foggy winter morning was still thick, mirroring the heaviness in my heart. Yet, I felt a renewed determination to face the day, knowing that I was doing everything I could to support my family.

I hurried through my morning chores, my hands trembling with a mix of dread and desperation. Every minute felt like an eternity. I packed his morning tea and some breakfast, hoping these small comforts would bring him some relief. The fog outside was dense, shrouding everything in a thick, gray mist, making the journey slow and challenging. My mind raced with worry as I navigated through the murky streets, each moment feeling more critical than the last.

Finally, I arrived at the hospital. The familiar surroundings did little to calm my nerves. I rushed to his floor, my heart pounding in my chest, every step echoing my growing apprehension. As I approached the caretaker, I struggled to keep my voice steady. "How is my dad?" I asked, my words tinged with a mix of desperation and hope.

The nurse looked at me with calm eyes and gently replied, "Hold on, don't panic. Your dad is fine. He's just sleeping. I kept his phone on silent because he couldn't sleep properly during the night."

A wave of relief engulfed me, easing some of the tension that had gripped me all morning. Yet, the worry lingered in the back of my mind. Knowing he was resting brought a fleeting moment of peace. I quietly entered his room, careful not to disturb his sleep. His bed was the first one in the ICU, and the sight of him sleeping peacefully was both comforting and heart-wrenching. I decided to let him rest and took a seat outside the ICU, my eyes scanning the monitors to check his vitals.

Donning the PPE kit, I found myself unavoidably reflecting on the challenges of life inside it. The suffocating feeling made me question if we were getting enough oxygen ourselves. I felt relieved that it was winter at least; otherwise, I couldn't imagine how people and doctors managed to wear this all day and night.

These thoughts made me appreciate the dedication of the healthcare workers even more, knowing they endured this daily to help others.

Sitting outside the ICU room, waiting for him to wake up, I reflected on the journey that had brought us here— Reflecting on how it all started and how COVID-19 has affected dad. Why did we initially ignore the signs of COVID-19, dismissing them as just a seasonal illness, and didn't get an RT-PCR test at the right time? Now, there's a profound sense of guilt. I regret every argument I had with dad, especially knowing he's usually right. The weight of these mistakes and missed opportunities for understanding weigh heavily on my heart, amplifying the apprehension and doubt we are all feeling now.

A few minutes later, the nurse came in and said, "It's tea and breakfast time. If you want to meet him, now's the time." I rushed to his side as he woke up. His eyes were tired, but he smiled when he saw me.

"Oh, you've come. I was waiting for you," he said.

"I was waiting for you to wake up," I replied. "Were you not able to sleep?"

As the nurse changed his nasal oxygen mask, he explained, "The beeping monitors, the oxygen mask, the hospital bed—all of it was uncomfortable. My constant focus on the monitor only deepened my sense of turmoil."

"Don't focus on that," I said gently. "There are other people to look at it. You just relax. That will help you get through this."

He agreed and then asked, "What's the status of my blood reports? Is it too bad? Am I critical? How much is the infection now, and how long will it take to cure? Will I be able to survive? What are the doctors saying?"

Despite being strong in this situation, I find myself wondering just how much COVID-19 can break a person and make them ask such questions. The relentless pressure, wary, and isolation have pushed me to the edge. I never imagined feeling so vulnerable and desperate. The pandemic's impact is profound, affecting even the strongest among us. The constant worry about my family's health and the lack of support makes each day feel like an invincible challenge.

I took a deep breath and said, "Your report is fine, dad. Yes, there is a high infection, but it's curable. With your will, optimistic thinking, and positivity, you'll get through this. You had bypass heart surgery, but all your lipid reports are fine, so there's nothing to worry about. You're fully vaccinated, and all your vitals are fine. You can see them yourself. You've never had problems before this, right? The main focus is on your lung infection, which will take time to heal, but you will be fine."

He smiled and replied, "I don't feel like I have a problem. I feel I could be normal. But everyone says I have a high infection rate and a high CT score, so I feel breathless. Without the oxygen mask, I can't breathe properly. That's the only problem. It will take time; nothing changes in one day."

I nodded in agreement and listened as he shared his thoughts. "If you face a problem in life, focus on solving it. Don't feel guilty, don't overthink, and don't stress about why it's happening. Situations happen; what matters is what you can do about them."

Dad is right, and indirectly, he is showing me the way. I need to focus on what I have in my hand right now, which is finding all possible ways to help improve dad's condition rather than regretting the past and overthinking the future. His guidance reminds me to concentrate on the present and take proactive steps to support him. This realization brings a sense of clarity and purpose, motivating me to do everything I can to make a difference.

As Lord Krishna says -

योगस्थः कुरु कर्माणि सङ्ग त्यक्त्वा धनञ्जय।

सद्धिध्यसद्धिध्योः समो भूत्वा समत्व योग उच्यतो। - Bhagwat Gita (chapter -2 verse 48)

When we understand that the effort is in our hands, not the results, we then focus only on doing our duty. The results are for the pleasure of God, and so we dedicate them to Him. If the results do not meet our expectations, we calmly accept them as the will of God.

I asked dad to rest and assured him I would visit again soon. I intentionally didn't mention bringing mom, hoping to surprise him. Otherwise, he wouldn't agree to let her come.

As I left the hospital and sat in the car while driving for a few minutes, reflecting on his words, I started creating a checklist for the next steps.

1. I need to be emotionally balanced for myself, my dad, and my family.

2. Arranging his regular physiotherapy sessions.

3. Consult with other doctors and hospitals about his reports.

4. Most importantly, don't lose hope.

I gathered myself and went home. As evening approached, my mom started preparing to visit the hospital. She hadn't seen my dad in almost three days, and the anticipation of the reunion filled her with a mix of excitement and worry. I made sure she had her mask and PPE kit, ensuring every measure was taken for her protection.

As mom dressed, the gravity of the situation hit her hard. Tears welled up in her eyes, and she began to sob, her shoulders shaking with each breath. Seeing her break down shattered the fragile resolve I had been clinging to, and I couldn't hold back my tears. We stood there, both overwhelmed by the sudden and harsh reality that had upended our lives. The weight of our dread, concerns, and powerlessness pressed down on us, making it difficult to breathe. At that moment, we were simply a mother and daughter, holding each other in a desperate attempt to find support amidst the chaos. The silent room echoed with our shared grief, each tear a proof of the love and puzzlement that now defined our days.

"Mom, I'm here," I said, my voice shaky but filled with determination. "Trust me, I will do my best for dad and you. Everything will be fine. Dad is handling this so bravely, and for his sake, we need to be strong too. You can't show your weakness in front of him."

I paused, taking a deep breath, feeling the weight of my words. "You are a strong lady; you've faced so many challenges in life with a smile. Remember the tough times you've conquered. Now, more than ever, we need that self-belief. Keep yourself together and be strong."

I held her hands tightly, feeling the warmth and love that had always been our anchor. Her tears slowed as she looked into my eyes, finding a spark of hope. We stood there, drawing trust from each other, knowing that our united front was the greatest support we could offer dad in his fight.

She nodded, wiping her tears and taking a deep breath to steady herself. Her shoulders, which had been trembling moments before, began to firm up. "You're right," she said, her voice regaining some firmness and determination. "I need to be strong for him."

I could see the shift in her eyes, a spark of tenacity reawakening. It was as if she was summoning all the courage and fortitude she had built over the years.

"Together, we'll get through this," I whispered, my resolve solidifying as I saw the change in her. We hugged each other tightly, drawing peace from our bond, ready to face the challenges ahead with renewed determination.

We left for the hospital, determined to put on a brave front. As we arrived, we found uncle and several other friends and relatives waiting, wanting to visit dad as well. The nurse managed to arrange a visit for mom. Before she went inside, I reminded her once more, "Be strong in front of him."

Inside, we discussed the circumstances of dad's illness. Everyone had their theories about how the infection had taken hold and why it had become so severe. After about thirty minutes, mom emerged from dad's room. Her expression was neutral, giving nothing away. I approached her, eager to know how the visit had gone.

"How was the meeting?" I asked, trying to read her face.

"It was good," she replied. "He seems better and more confident. I insisted he keep up with his exercises more often because it's important for his recovery, but he's not doing them properly."

"Don't worry," I assured her. "I'll make sure he does them. He'll listen to me."

As we prepared to leave, mom shared more about the visit. "Dad was surprised to see me. He was happy and concerned. He asked why I came and told me I should stay at home."

"I wanted to see you," she had told him. "I'm fine now, and I really needed to see you in person."

We talked about how, for a while, she should continue to see him via video call to minimize exposure. She agreed, understanding the necessity of precautions, even though the desire to be close to him was strong.

"Dad was a bit emotional," she said softly. "He apologized for so many things. He said, 'Intentionally or unintentionally, I've made many mistakes in life, and I want to apologize. I don't want to live with regret.' I told him it's okay. We are all human, and no one is perfect. I told him not to think negatively but to live positively."

As we reached home, I noticed a sense of peace on my mom's face that hadn't been there before. Seeing dad had given her some peace of mind, and she seemed more at ease. The day had been emotionally exhausting, but the faith we found in each other made us ready to face whatever lay ahead.

I went to bed feeling a bit tired but determined. I told myself, "You have to be strong. This is a challenge, a chapter in your life to test your capabilities. Get through this with grace, love, and positivity." I prayed for my father before sleeping and finally drifted off.

DAY Four: Finding Strength in the Fight

At 6:00 AM, I woke up from another restless night. These days, I hardly get any sound sleep. Even when I do manage to sleep, my thoughts are consumed by worry for my dad. I constantly wonder what he might be doing and whether he's able to sleep properly.

Sitting on the edge of my bed, sipping water, I found myself reflecting on how much I've changed over the past few days. The weight of the situation has forced me to discover a robustness I never knew I had. I never imagined that I would have to face such a challenging situation so early in life. Yet, here I am, managing to hold it together.

As I pondered these changes, I realized that life's toughest tests often reveal our hidden capabilities. It's as if God, in presenting these challenges, also provides us with the stamina to endure them. This thought brought me a small measure of comfort. Despite the immense pressure and inner turmoil, I found a spark of hope within me—a belief that perhaps I was strong enough to pass this test.

Thinking about all this, I have to continue to believe that we will come out of this stronger and more united than ever. With a deep breath, I prepared to face another day, carrying the hope and perseverance that had slowly been building within me.

I knew I had many chores to complete today, so I asked my mom and cousin to visit my dad in the morning while I focused on making the necessary arrangements. The hospital's limited availability for therapy had been frustrating, so I decided to hire an outside therapist.

To stay organized, I made a detailed checklist for the day. This included following up with the therapist, contacting the specialist, and ensuring that everything my dad needed was prepared and ready. Knowing that I had a busy day ahead, I sat down with my mom and cousin to have morning tea. This ritual had become a cornerstone of our daily routine, offering a moment of peace and relaxation before the day's chaos unfolded.

As we sipped our tea, I felt a wave of comfort enveloped me. The warmth of the tea and the presence of my family gave me the strength to face the challenges ahead. My mom received calls asking about dad's health, and she updated everyone, narrating the whole situation up to now. My brother also joined us for tea. It was a small family gathering, currently filled with a mix of emotions. We talked about our plans for the day and the small victories we had achieved so far.

Soon, mom recounted a fond memory of my dad, reminiscing about how he always enjoyed such tea conversations. He loves talking about life, sharing updates on everything, and planning for the day ahead.

With the morning tea finished, I took a deep breath and mentally prepared myself for the tasks ahead. It was

9:00 AM, and I was busy calling various therapists and specialists in pulmonology. My phone buzzed with a video call from the hospital. It was my dad.

"Why haven't you come today?" he asked, a hint of worry in his voice.

"I'm arranging a few things that are needed, dad. I'll come in the late afternoon," I replied. I checked on his health and reminded him to take care of himself. He seemed convinced but was unusually silent. "Mom and my brother will be coming to visit you, so don't worry. After finishing a few things, I'll come to visit you, too."

He responded, "No worries, take your time. See you in the evening!"

By 3:00 PM, I had found a good therapist who could start visiting the hospital to provide therapy that very day. I also secured an appointment with a reputable pulmonologist for the next day and had already sent all my dad's reports for review. Discussing things with my uncle, he was also trying to arrange things over the phone. After completing these crucial obligations, I headed home to rest for a bit.

At 5:30 PM, the therapist called me to inform me that he would be reaching the hospital soon and needed everything arranged so he could start the session at 6:00 PM. I rushed to the hospital; my mind focused on ensuring everything was in place for my dad's treatment.

As I reached the hospital reception, the receptionist called out my last name, "Are you from the Gaur family?"

"Yes," I replied, stepping closer.

"I heard you have family members who tested positive for COVID-19. I have the results of the RT-PCR tests," she said, handing me the reports. My heart sank as I glanced at the results—it was my uncle's and cousin's reports, and both were positive. I immediately called them to confirm. They told me they had seen the results online and were planning to quarantine themselves completely. This was another blow. With them in quarantine, there would be no one to help me, and I could only hope that their health would remain stable. "Take care of yourselves," I urged them, trying to keep my voice calm.

With a heavy heart, I moved forward to my dad's room. The weight of the day's events pressed on me. As I entered, I took a deep breath, pushing my worries aside, ready to focus on supporting my dad through his therapy session and the challenges ahead.

As I entered the ICU room, I saw him sitting on his bed, deep in thoughts. He looked at me instantly, and I missed this usual smile on his face.

"How has your day been so far?" I asked.

"It was good. I did a video call with my friends today. It was motivating when they said I would be home soon and we could plan a trip together," he said, looking genuinely happy.

"What did you eat? How are you feeling now?" I asked, my concern evident in my voice as I sat beside my dad's bed, hoping to gauge his well-being from his response.

He gave me a weary smile and replied, "I'm fine, just tired of spending time on this hospital bed and in this environment. I want to be at home, surrounded by family. But I understand why I need to be here right now."

His words hung in the air, laden with a mix of resignation and hope. I could see the fatigue in his eyes, the longing for the familiar comfort of home. The sterile hospital room, with its beeping machines and antiseptic smell, was a sharp contrast to the warmth of our home.

"I miss the simple things," he continued, his voice softening. "The morning tea, the chatter at the breakfast table, just being around you all. So, I'm praying and hoping to be home soon. I'm keeping my will strong and my thoughts positive. That's what's keeping me going."

I felt a surge of admiration for him. Even in this difficult time, he is focusing on the positives, maintaining his resolve to fight through the illness.

"We miss you at home too, dad," I said, putting my hand on his shoulder gently. "And we're all here, doing everything we can to get you back home soon. Just keep that hope alive, and we'll get through this."

He nodded, a small, calming smile playing on his lips. "I know, and that means everything to me."

He started sharing stories about his past, about how he survived three major heart attacks in his early 40s. It was a tough time for him and our family. He lost twenty-two kilograms during that period and spent two months in the hospital.

That was a tough time for everyone. My grandparents were also there. When he was admitted to the hospital for two months for bypass surgery, we witnessed the courage and positivity he showed. Despite the challenges, he fought through everything, proving how resilient he truly is. His spirit during that period remains an inspiration to all of us.

"I've been through so much, and I'm not afraid of what's ahead. I am ready to fight," he said, tears in his eyes.

Listening to him, I felt incredibly blessed. "Life is tough, but you are tougher, dad," he reminded me. I was so proud of him and hoped to have even half his courage and motivation.

While we were talking, the physiotherapist arrived in the ICU room, having completed all the necessary formalities at the desk. His presence brought a sense of hope. He greeted us warmly before carefully examining my dad's reports and checking his vitals. My dad, despite his fatigue, greeted the therapist with a determined nod.

The therapist began his session with a steady confidence. He guided my dad through a series of exercises, explaining each step with patience and clarity. I could see my dad putting in every ounce of effort, his face set with determination. The therapist's encouraging words seemed to revitalize him, and for the first time in days, I saw a spark of vitality in his eyes.

After the session, the therapist turned to me, his expression both serious and encouraging. "He has a high CT score," he said, acknowledging the gravity of my dad's condition. "It's critical, but he's active and willing to recover. His determination is remarkable, and that's a big part of the battle."

I listened intently, absorbing his words. The weight of the situation pressed down on me, but the therapist's positive outlook offered a glimmer of hope. "With daily sessions, he'll get better soon," the therapist continued. "Consistency is key. We'll work on his strength and lung capacity. He's responding well, and that's a very good sign."

I felt a surge of gratitude for the therapist's expertise and kindness. My dad's willingness to push through his exhaustion and fight for his recovery is inspiring. "Thank you," I said, my voice steady but filled with emotion.

The therapist nodded, giving my dad an encouraging pat on the shoulder. "You're doing great," he said to my dad. "Keep up the good work, and we'll see improvements soon."

As the therapist left, I turned back to my dad, who looked both tired and hopeful. "You hear that, dad? You're doing great," I said, holding his hand gently.

He smiled a weary but genuine smile. "I know. I'll keep fighting," he replied, his voice resolute.

I told him to rest and prepared to leave. Before stepping away, he reached out with a voice tinged with vulnerability, asking, 'Can you come in the morning?' he asked. "I feel anxious and scared during the cleaning routine when I have to remove my mask several times."

His words hit me hard. "Of course, dad," I assured him I'd be here. You don't have to worry."

He nodded, a flicker of relief crossing his face. "Could you also arrange for the Lord Hanuman's Sundarkand path to be played? It always gives me a sense of positivity."

"Absolutely," I promised, immediately making arrangements with the hospital staff to play the Sundarkand path whenever he needed it on his phone using headphones. It was a small but significant gesture to keep his spirits high.

After a long, tiring day, I drove home, my mind heavy with the weight of the day's events and the tasks that lay ahead. Each turn of the wheel was a reminder of the responsibilities I had shouldered. As I navigated the familiar streets, My priority was clear: to see my dad improving every day and to spend as much time with him as possible. I believed deeply in the power of family support—it often works wonders, sometimes even more than medicine.

Once home, the quiet of the night wrapped around me like a heavy blanket. Before slipping into bed, I updated my mom about dad's visit while having dinner. Later, I took a moment to pray, my heart filled with both hope and worry. I prayed for my dad's recovery and for the strength to support him and our family through this challenging time. The day's exhaustion settled into my bones, but so did a renewed sense of purpose.

DAY Five: A Day of Hope and Reflection

I woke up to the sound of a video call ringing from the hospital. It was 7:30 AM, and I realized with a start that I had missed the first call. Heart pounding, I quickly called back. To my immense relief, my dad answered immediately, looking positively radiant. His smile was so genuine and warm.

"Did you sleep well?" He asked, his voice tinged with concern.

"Yes, I slept early yesterday," I replied. "How about you, dad?" I asked, still in a sleepy voice. "I was tired from the physiotherapy, so I went to bed early. It was a sound sleep." His eyes sparkled with energy as he continued, "I woke up early and listened to the Sundarkand path for two hours. It filled me with such positivity. I'm feeling fresh and positive today."

His words soothed me like a balm, soothing my worries. The thought of him engaging with something that brought him comfort and peace made me feel that, despite the hospital environment, he was finding ways to heal and stay strong. His renewed energy and enthusiasm were noticeable, radiating through the screen and lifting my spirits.

"That's wonderful, dad," I said. "Hearing you so positive gives me a lot of hope. Keep this up. We'll get through this together."

As we continued to chat, the morning light filtered through my window, casting a gentle glow in the room. It felt symbolic, as if this day, filled with renewed hope and optimism, was breaking through the fog of the past weeks. His perseverance and determination were infectious, reminding me of the strength we all carry within us. I resolved to hold onto this positivity with the same courage and optimism that my dad was displaying.

He asked about his brother, mentioning that he hadn't seen him the previous evening. "Is everything okay?" he inquired, his brow furrowing with concern.

"Sorry, I forgot to mention it yesterday," I said, feeling a pang of guilt. "Uncle and sister tested positive for COVID. They're both completely fine, but they have to quarantine themselves."

His face tightened with worry, but he quickly composed himself. "Make sure they take proper precautions," he advised, his voice steady but serious. "If symptoms persist, they should start treatment early."

"I've already spoken to them," I steadied him. "They're taking all the necessary steps. Don't worry; everything is under control."

He nodded, relief evident in his eyes, but his concern quickly shifted. "And your mom? How is she?"

"She's fine," I replied, making an effort to sound as supportive as possible.

"Good," he said. "Don't bring her to the hospital now. She needs to rest at home for a while. And you, please take care of yourself. Make sure to take all necessary precautions when you come here. Try not to come too often."

I nodded, appreciating his concern for us, even in his condition. "I will, dad. And I wanted to let you know that your latest RT-PCR report came back negative. You're no longer infected. We're just dealing with the post-covid effects."

A look of relief spread across his face. "That's good to hear," he said, a hint of a smile returning. "Don't worry, things will be fine."

During our call, mom joined to see dad. "How are you?" she asked, her voice full of concern.

"I'm fine," dad replied. "Don't come to the hospital. Stay home and rest."

"Okay," she said, reluctantly agreeing. "Everyone is concerned about you."

"No need to worry too much, whatever is meant to happen will happen. Take care of yourself," he said with hope and love.

Dad then turned to me. "Are you coming, Naina?"

"Yes, I will come," I assured him.

Just then, dad removed his oxygen mask and began his breathing exercises. To our surprise and delight, his oxygen levels held steady at 89%, a significant improvement. We were all thrilled to see this progress.

At 9:00 AM, I left home and headed to the hospital. I arrived just in time to see dad, who was eager to share how much better he was feeling. The physiotherapy had made him feel more positive and had even improved his appetite. He was maintaining good oxygen levels without the mask, which was an encouraging sign. We sat together and enjoyed tea and breakfast, savoring the small victories.

While we were talking, I remembered the appointment with another doctor for a second opinion. Seeing dad in such a stable state, I felt comfortable stepping out briefly. When I mentioned that I would come back in the evening and bring the therapist with me, he nodded quickly, his eyes filled with understanding and trust.

I left the room and soon received a call from the specialist. After reviewing dad's reports, the doctor emphasized the importance of closely monitoring his D-dimer levels due to his history of heart surgery. He recommended another CT scan in a day or two to check for any progress. Uplifted by this advice, I felt a mix of relief and determination.

As I made my way back home, I thought about the many ways our lives had changed so suddenly. The specialist's guidance gave me a clearer direction, and knowing that we were taking all the necessary steps for dad's recovery brought a semblance of peace to my restless mind.

When we arrived at the hospital in the evening, I found dad sleeping deeply. Although I hesitated to disturb him, the physiotherapist needed to start the session. Gently, I touched his shoulder. Dad woke up, saw me, smiled, and waved. That smile was everything to me, a beacon of hope in these trying times.

The physiotherapist began the session, working patiently with dad.

After the session, I returned to dad's room, where he was resting peacefully. I sat down beside him and gently asked, "How are you feeling now, dad?"

He looked at me with a smile, "I feel okay right now," he replied, his voice steady and calm.

Recovery takes time, and I'm prepared for that. I understand it's a gradual process, but with every passing day, I feel a bit stronger.

We continued our conversation, and dad began sharing stories from his past, his eyes twinkling with a mix of nostalgia and humor. He chuckled softly as he confessed, *"I learned some things a bit late in life. I made many mistakes and wrong decisions. It's crucial to ask yourself where your life is going. If you don't stop and reflect, you build regret. Seeing your life as a third person helps you understand your actions without bias."*

I nodded, deeply impressed by his wisdom. "You're right, dad. We all make mistakes, but it's about how quickly we recover and learn from them."

He continued, "Because of my bad habits of smoking and drinking, I needed an early bypass surgery and faced many health-related issues. Even taking on family responsibilities came late to me. But looking back, everything is connected, and each incident teaches a lesson. It's important to review your life regularly and make necessary changes at the right time."

Moved by his words, I felt a deep sense of pride and admiration. "I'm proud of you, dad. We all make mistakes, but we can learn and adapt to those matters."

His eyes softened as he smiled at me. "Thank you, beta. Life is a journey of continuous learning. We need to embrace our past, learn from it, and move forward with a positive outlook."

As he spoke, I realized how much he had grown and how his experiences had shaped him into the wise man before me. His reflections were not just about his past mistakes but also about the importance of adaptability, growth, and the power of self-awareness. This conversation was a profound reminder that every moment, every decision, and every mistake is part of a larger tapestry of life, teaching us and molding us into better versions of ourselves.

I took dad's phone to save the numbers of the hospital staff. As I was checking his phone, sitting next to him, I noticed a series of selfies he had taken with his mask on, striking different poses. Laughing, I asked him humorously, "dad, are you taking selfies here?"

He replied with a grin, "Yes, why not? This is also part of my life." He explained that he also sent these photos to his friends to inform them that he was admitted to the hospital.

As I looked through his chats, I couldn't stop myself from laughing. Soon, he joined in, His laughter was full of life. "Life is already too boring," he said. "There should be no lack of fun in any situation."

At that moment, we both forgot all our worries. The room, filled with our laughter, felt lighter, and for a while, it was just us enjoying a simple, joyful moment amidst the chaos.

Soon, I encouraged him to do his breathing exercises and have a protein-rich snack. As I prepared to leave, I could see he didn't want me to go. He cherished these moments with family, finding strength in our presence.

I asked dad if he needed anything else and promised him, "I'll come back in the morning, dad. I should leave now."

He looked at me with a comforting smile and said, "OK, take care, and don't worry about me. Have a sound sleep."

Driving home, I tried to relax by putting on some music and taking a moment for myself. After that, I completed the necessary shopping before heading home.

At home, mom could tell how dad was doing just by looking at me. I updated her about dad's health and how he was getting stronger, knowing it would lift her spirits. After spending some time with family, I prayed for dad and for everyone's strength. Exhausted but hopeful, I fell asleep, wishing for a better tomorrow.

DAY Six: Choices and Destiny

Today, I woke up early, around 5:50 AM, but the tiredness in my bones and the gloomy weather outside kept me in bed. I rolled over, my mind full of questions. "Is life a matter of choice, or is it all destined?" I wondered. For the past two years, the whole world has faced the relentless impact of COVID-19. Every third person seemed to get infected. My parents were very careful with precautions and stayed safe during the peak of the pandemic. Yet now, when infections are rare, and most people recover quickly, my dad is hospitalized and critically ill. Was this meant to be?

Lord Krishna says -

चातुर्वर्ण्यं मया सृष्टं गुणकर्मविभागशः ।
तस्य कर्तारमपि मां विद्ध्यकर्तारमव्ययम् ॥

The Lord is the creator of everything. Everything is born of Him, everything is sustained by Him, and everything, after annihilation, rests in Him. He is, therefore, the creator of the four divisions of the social order and life. – Bhagwat Gita chapter 4. Division13

With these thoughts swirling in my mind, I forced myself out of bed, feeling the weight of my worries. I called the hospital for an update on dad. The attendant informed me that dad hadn't slept well last night due to discomfort but was now resting. He also mentioned that the Chief Minister was visiting the hospital today, which had everyone excited, including my dad, a big political fan. Visitors were not allowed during breakfast time due to the visit, but I managed to see dad over a video call. He waved and said he was fine, his excitement about the political leader's visit evident. It was a brief update call on his health.

After a while of managing tasks at home with my mom, around 11:30 AM, I decided to go to the hospital. As I quietly entered ICU, I was greeted by a sight that lifted my spirits: Dad looked fresh and energized, His eyes sparkled with a contagious liveliness.

"How are you feeling? How's your morning been?" I asked, setting the tea down beside him.

He seemed almost to forget about the oxygen mask strapped to his face as he launched into an animated account of his morning. "You'll never believe who I saw! The Chief Minister was walking just outside my room. The hallway was buzzing with activity," he said, his excitement pronounced.

We chatted about politics, his enthusiasm momentarily eclipsing the reality of his condition. Our conversation was abruptly interrupted when the doctor arrived for his daily check-in. The doctor suggested dad incorporate some additions into his routine, such as hourly breathing exercises and taking steam. His tone was gentle, but it was clear he was gently admonishing dad for not taking an active role in his recovery.

I turned to dad, my voice sharper than I intended. "You need to take this seriously, every minute counts. You can't afford to skip these exercises." I could see the numbers on the oximeter flicker slightly downward, but they remained within a safe range, offering some relief. Dad agreed to follow the doctor's advice more proactively now.

Despite the tense moment, dad's determination shone through. He wanted to video call the rest of the family, eager to share his progress. As he also demonstrated his breathing exercises over a video call, his face lit up with genuine happiness. The joy in his eyes and voice was a good sign, a small but significant victory in these trying times.

As I watched him interact with the family, the same question nagged at me: Is life a choice or destiny? After he ended the call, I asked dad the same question. His response was profound. *"Life is about how you create it and how you react to different situations. In good or bad times, you always have a choice: you can become depressed, overthink, and feel guilty, or you can learn from it, move on, and build your life from those lessons. Never give up. Enjoy the good times to the fullest and make the best of them. Help others whenever and wherever you can. That's what I believe. Become a better person each day. One day, you'll know what's best for you. When that time comes, nothing can shake you because a ship doesn't sink because of the water around it; it sinks when the water gets inside.' Most importantly, embrace what you have right now."*

His words resonated deeply with me. Everything started to make sense. The nurse came in, reminding me to leave as visiting hours were over. I asked dad to rest and promised to return for dinner. As I walked out, I pondered over how people are so busy chasing ambitions, often forgetting the contingency of life. We should do what we want and be prepared for whatever comes next.

With these thoughts, I headed home. The realization that life is unpredictable yet filled with choices gave me a new perspective. For dinner, I would return to the hospital, as dad had asked. It was these moments together that mattered the most, and I was determined to cherish each one.

As the clock struck 7:00 PM, my mother was engrossed in preparing dinner for dad, who had made a special request. Amid this routine, I received an unexpected call from the hospital informing me that dad was eagerly awaiting his meal. With a sense of urgency, I quickly rallied my brother, and together, we set off, bearing the meal that mom had lovingly prepared.

Upon our arrival at the ICU, we were met with an unexpected obstacle. We were stopped at the entrance, unable to go any further. Inside, an urgent emergency was unfolding. A critically ill patient was surrounded by a team of specialists, and their focused efforts were clear even from a distance. The atmosphere was tense, filled with a sense of urgency.

Outside, the scene was just as intense. The patient's family stood together, their faces full of apprehension and unease. Each moment felt like an eternity as they awaited news about their loved one. The burden of their concern was heavy, casting a somber shadow over the bustling hospital corridor.

As I stood there, I felt a deep empathy for the family, their distress mirroring my own. It was a stark reminder of life's fragility and the unpredictability of fate. I silently prayed for the patient's recovery, hoping their ordeal would soon end.

My thoughts wandered to dad. During the emergency, he likely sat unaware, eagerly awaiting his dinner. Behind his closed room door, he was shielded from the turmoil outside. I couldn't shake the worry about how he was coping with the unsettling sights and sounds around him.

Time seemed to drag on as we waited for news from the ICU. Finally, the doctor emerged, his face filled with concern. The anxious family members crowded around him, their questions pouring out desperately. Amid the chaos, I caught parts of the grim update. The patient's infection had caused a blockage in his airway, requiring an emergency procedure to help him breathe. Each word felt like a blow, leaving me feeling weak and vulnerable.

My brother and I exchanged a glance, sharing a mutual feeling of dread and trepidation. We had never encountered such a dire situation before, and the weight of it left us speechless. A lump formed in my throat, and I felt an urgent thirst, but there was no water available. We were left to grapple with our fears in silence, hoping for a positive outcome.

The tension increased as the doctor administered a high dose of medication, a last effort to save the patient. We held our breath, praying for a miraculous turnaround. Moments later, the nurse delivered the devastating news—the patient had passed away. The weight of the words was heavy, sending shockwaves through the tense atmosphere.

The grief that swept through the family was heartbreaking, their cries echoing down the hallway. It was a stark reminder of the toll the pandemic had taken on so many lives. In that moment of profound loss, our hearts went out to them, but we were powerless to offer any real comfort. The constraints of the pandemic limited our ability to console them as we wished. All we could do was witness their pain and offer small words of comfort, knowing it would never be enough to ease their sorrow.

Finally permitted entry, we approached dad with heavy hearts, the recent tragedy casting a mournful shadow over our reunion. His eyes, weary yet relieved to see us, spoke volumes of the turmoil he had endured. With a heavy heart, he recounted the distressing events, his voice weighed down by the gravity of what he had witnessed. In an attempt to offer comfort, I was hoping to shift his focus away from the trauma he had witnessed, even if only momentarily.

Despite our earlier excitement about the specially prepared dinner, the room was heavy with sorrow. Dad, visibly shaken by the ordeal, had lost his appetite. Still, knowing he needed to keep his strength up, I gently urged him to eat, coaxing him to take a few reluctant bites. The joy that had initially accompanied the meal was gone, overshadowed by the lingering sadness.

To lift his spirits, we engaged in conversation, trying to provide him with a brief escape from the tragedy. As I gently massaged his head to soothe the ache caused by the constant presence of the oxygen mask, my brother tenderly tended to his cold feet, offering a small gesture of comfort. Gradually, the tension began to ease, replaced by a bit of calm.

Before leaving, we made sure dad was comfortable, lingering for a moment to exchange glances full of silent consolation. As we left the room, carrying the half-eaten meal, a sense of heaviness remained, a gentle reminder of life's fragility and the enduring strength of the human spirit.

As dad said goodnight, telling us to go home quickly and rest, we agreed, saying our final goodnight before heading home. Yet, as we retraced our steps, the weight of the day's events was heavily upon us. The morning started with hope but ended with a sharp reminder of how unpredictable life can be.

The profound impact it had on the grieving family resonated deeply within us. As we were heading home, the echoes of their grief reverberated in my mind, haunting me with a sense of helplessness.

Despite our best efforts, we were powerless to alter the course of events and were left to grapple with the profound sorrow that enveloped us. The contrast between brief moments of happiness and underlying tragedy left a lasting impact, strongly reminding us of life's impermanence.

Back home, I tried to shake off the day's heaviness. I prayed for dad, our family, and everyone struggling through these challenging times.

Exhausted, I fell asleep, hoping for a better tomorrow.

DAY Seven: A Day of Ambiguity

I slept deeply last night, exhausted from the emotional rollercoaster of the previous day. But the respite was short-lived. It was 8:00 AM when my mother woke me, her voice trembling as she handed me the phone. It was from the hospital. My heart raced as I answered.

"Your dad's oxygen levels have dropped suddenly," the nurse said. "He was panicking a bit because of a cough he had since early morning, but he is stable now. We need to do a CT scan today."

jitters spiked through me. I asked if I could come in soon, and they assured me to take my time as he was stable. I hung up, feeling a wave of dread. My mom started asking for an update on dad's health and about the call I received from the hospital. I told her everything was fine, just some fluctuations in his oxygen levels, which is expected. Mom was quietly listening to this.

I sat quietly on my bed, processing the situation. Memories of the previous night's tragedy at the hospital flooded back, and I felt drained and lost. Unable to hold myself together, I went to the bathroom, closed the door, and broke down. I wept quietly, allowing the anguish, distress, and helplessness to pour out. It was the only place I could truly release my emotions, hidden from my mother's troubled gaze.

After a while, I composed myself and gathered my thoughts. I called my uncle and asked him to meet us at the hospital. Despite knowing he was COVID-positive, I felt we might need his support, even if it had to be from a distance. I encouraged my mom, put together dad's morning tea, and left for the hospital with a heavy heart. The drive felt unbearably long, each moment filled with a mix of intimidation and hope.

When I arrived at the ICU, the tension was obvious. He was coughing and struggling to speak, each breath a struggle. Each cough seemed to lower his oxygen levels on the monitor, clearly showing his fragility. It was heartbreaking to see him, once so strong and vibrant, now so frail. The beeping machines and the sterile hospital environment only highlighted his vulnerability.

"Are you okay, dad?" I asked gently.

"I'm fine," he managed to say between coughs. "Just this cough since last night."

The nurse updated me on his condition, and I nodded, absorbing every detail while my heart pounded in my chest.

I handed him the tea, our usual comforting ritual, hoping it would lend a sense of normality to the situation. As he sipped, I reminded him gently but firmly about the importance of staying calm and following the doctor's instructions.

I noticed a file beside dad's bed and, unable to ignore it, picked it up to look. My heart sank as I read through the results: Dad's assuring words didn't match his actual condition. The tests showed a significant drop in his oxygen levels and elevated D-dimer levels, indicating the presence of blood clots. The doctors had increased his oxygen intake, which meant the progress we thought he had been making was being undone.

Seeing this stark reality laid out in the test results, I felt a wave of panic overwhelm me. I tried to maintain my composure, though my legs were trembling beneath me. I turned to dad, who was uncomfortable breathing and speaking and gently took his hand. "Dad, let's focus on taking deep breaths and try not to talk too much," I said, my voice steady despite the turmoil inside me.

As he attempted to follow my instructions, I could see the effort it took him. The fortitude that had always defined him seemed to falter, and it was heartbreaking to witness. I inhaled deeply, attempting to calm my nerves, and focused on being there for him, offering what little comfort I could amid our shared turmoil.

"You're going to be okay, dad," I said, forcing a smile. "You're in good hands."

He gestured weakly, asking about his oxygen levels. I assured him he was fine, even as the monitor showed otherwise. I closed his eyes gently, hoping he could relax a bit.

My uncle arrived shortly, clad in a PPE kit, his presence a balm to our frayed nerves. Together, we supported Dad, offering a serene presence and engaging in conversation to keep his mind occupied and free from worry. We spoke softly about family memories and plans, anything to keep his mind off his struggle for breath. Our combined presence seemed to soothe him, if only a little.

Stepping out of the ICU, I felt the weight of the situation pressing down harder. I turned to my uncle, his eyes mirroring my concern, and we began discussing dad's condition. We both agreed that the current hospital wasn't providing the improvements we had hoped for. The events of the previous night still lingered in my mind, casting a shadow of doubt and negativity over the place. Dad's worsening condition only intensified my concern.

"We need to move dad to a different hospital," I said firmly.

I mentioned the pulmonary specialist I had been consulting, renowned for his work with COVID patients and boasting a high success rate. Soon, my uncle agreed, recognizing the urgency of the situation. We decided to call the specialist, and after a tense discussion about dad's current status, he agreed to take him on as a patient at another hospital in town. He wanted to conduct more tests and urgent CT scans to get a comprehensive understanding of dad's condition.

As we arranged for the transfer, a sense of cautious hope began to take root. Moving dad was a risk, but it felt like a necessary one. We couldn't afford to stay stagnant; we needed to fight for his recovery with every resource available. I prayed this decision would bring the turnaround we so desperately needed.

After we all agreed and planned for the transfer, I explained the plan to dad. After asking a few questions, he also agreed to the transfer.

I finally took leave from work, having managed to juggle responsibilities amid the chaos until now. Explaining the situation to my boss, I made it clear that there was no time for distractions; I needed to focus entirely on dad.

The process of transferring hospitals was long and fraught with red tape. My uncle handled the paperwork while I stayed close to dad, not wanting to leave him for a second. If I couldn't be with him, I made sure someone from the family was there. This was our new reality—constant vigilance and support.

By 5:00 PM, we were finally ready to move dad to the new hospital. The day had been a whirlwind of tension, decisions, and preparations. I watched Dad, lying in his bed and softly mumbling the prayer. The future was unpredictable, but we had to hold on to hope for a better outcome.

The ambulance approached after thirty minutes, its siren a haunting reminder of our urgent situation. My brother and uncle were there, ready to assist in transferring dad. The paramedics brought in a stretcher, and I could see the panic in dad's eyes. He tried to mask it with confidence, but the unassertiveness was evident.

The doctor and nurse asked dad to move to the stretcher. In a hurried attempt, he got up quickly, trying to sit on the stretcher without assistance. His sudden movement took everyone by surprise. As soon as he settled on the stretcher, he started gasping for breath. His oxygen levels plummeted, and his face turned a frightening shade of red.

Panic spread through the room. The doctor and nurses rushed to his side, adjusting his oxygen supply. I stood there, holding dad's hand, feeling utterly helpless. His hand, usually warm and strong, was now as cold as ice. My palm was wet with sweat and trembling uncontrollably. I was trying to hold myself together, but my mind was paralyzed with worry.

My uncle, seeing the gravity of the situation, quickly spoke up. "We can't move him like this," he said, his voice steady but tinged with panic. Everyone nodded in agreement. Dad was visibly struggling for oxygen, his breaths shallow and labored.

The doctors worked quickly, adjusting the oxygen cylinder and trying to stabilize him. I watched in agony as my father, my hero, the man who had always been my strength, lay there helpless. He had lost so much weight in just a week, and seeing him fight for something as basic as oxygen was heart-wrenching.

The room was tense, filled with the beeping of monitors and the hushed voices of the medical staff. At that moment, I couldn't hold my emotions and hid behind my sister's back, crying silently, trembling because of this situation. She held me, her own eyes teary. This lion of a man, who had always been so full of life and vigor, was now struggling to survive.

At that moment, time seemed to stand still. The only thing that mattered was making sure dad could breathe normally. The transfer was put on hold, and the medical team worked tirelessly to stabilize him. All I could do was pray and hope for his recovery, holding onto his hand and silently willing him to stay strong.

They shifted dad back to his bed, assisted by the nurse and staff. As dad settled back, we were asked to wait outside. I kept sneaking peeks into the room, watching the doctors administer back-to-back injections and medications. Dad seemed in shock, unable to believe what had just happened. He looked terrified.

The doctor came out, and we anxiously asked about dad's condition. "Right now, stabilizing him is our priority," he said. "We'll constantly monitor him and make sure he's fine. We need to run immediate tests to find out what happened. This could be a case of post-covid side effects or lung fibrosis." As the doctor spoke, my eyes kept darting to the monitor displaying dad's oxygen levels and vital signs. Dad lay there, eyes closed, trying to regain his strength. I could see his determination.

I requested the doctor to let my brother and me stay at the hospital overnight while everyone else left. I didn't want to leave dad alone. It was already late, and the doctor, understanding the urgency and the events of the previous night, agreed to let us stay. We wouldn't be leaving the hospital until the next day.

Peeking into the room, I saw dad opening his eyes and looking for us. I waved, and he nodded for me to come in. Approaching him with the doctor, we were reminded that dad shouldn't speak much. When asked if he wanted to eat, dad initially refused. However, with some insistence from both the doctor and me, he agreed to eat a little, understanding the need for sustenance given the strong medications he was on.

"I'm in shock to see my body like this," dad said weakly. "I've given up on my body in just a week. What has happened?"

"It's just a phase, dad, not permanent," I swiftly calmed him

. "You are getting proper treatment and you will be fine." Despite feeling sleepy and dizzy, he managed to eat a little. We encouraged him to rest. My brother and I, rubbing his head and massaging his cold hands and feet. It was going to be a long night.

The doctor arranged a place for us to sit and sleep next to dad's room. My brother and I took turns monitoring the vital signs from outside. The night was more than half gone, and neither of us was in the mood to rest. We ate some food that mom had sent from home and continued our vigil, taking turns to keep an eye on the monitor.

Around 3 AM, I saw dad sitting up. I waved and gestured to ask if he couldn't sleep. He shook his head, indicating he was fine but felt like sitting for a while. We exchanged a look, both of us feeling helpless, bound by the situation. It struck me that no matter how strong a person is, life has its way of playing with you. Even the strongest can be rendered helpless by life's unpredictable turns.

After dad lay down again, my brother urged me to get some rest. Around 4:00 AM, I was half asleep when I noticed dad's oxygen level on the monitor drop to thirty-five. My brother and I panicked and rushed to the nurse. She came in to check, finding dad sleeping peacefully. It turned out the loose oximeter on his finger had caused the false alarm. We made sure everything was secure and then sat down again, hearts still racing.

We continued our quiet observance, my eyes heavy with exhaustion and worry. I prayed for this ordeal to pass as quickly as possible, hoping for a better day ahead.

DAY Eight: Wrestling with Fate

As the restless night gave way to dawn, we both slept for a while. It was 6:30 AM when I woke up, and after a few seconds, I found myself drawn back to my father's room, unable to find respite in slumber. There he lay, his eyes searching for familiar faces, his expression a mix of yearning and unease. Upon spotting me, he beckoned me closer, his voice laced with concern. "Why did you stay here yesterday? You should have gone home to rest," he implored, his paternal instincts overriding his discomfort.

Alleviating his worries about our well-being, I assured him, only to be confronted with a heart-wrenching confession. "Last night was a nightmare," he confided, his voice faltering. "I thought today might be my last day." The weight of those words hung heavily in the air.

Refusing to entertain such despair, I rallied my spirits, reminding him of the profound impact his might had on those around him. "You are an inspiration to many," I declared, my voice brimming with conviction. "How could you even consider surrender? You must keep your spirit high, for that is the wellspring of your recovery and our collective joy."

Sensing his need for comfort, he asked for the familiar melodies of the Sundarkanth Path, the devotional hymns that had always vigored his beliefs. Without hesitation, I played the sacred verses just as the first rays of the rising sun came through the windows, signaling a new day and a fresh start.

As the mantras enveloped us, I witnessed a remarkable transformation unfold before my eyes. With each recitation, each gentle clap of his hands, my father's posture straightened, his countenance radiating a renewed strength and unwavering faith. In that moment, the burdens that had weighed upon us seemed to dissipate, replaced by an overwhelming sense of relief and gratitude.

My thoughts were immediately drawn back to my father's room. Despite the exhaustion from sleepless nights and constant stress, I found peace in witnessing his unwavering courage. It amazed me how he embraced joy even in the face of adversity.

I silently prayed for his recovery, feeling grateful for being by his side during this tough journey. If I had stayed in Germany, separated from him, I would have been consumed by regret. But here I was, an essential part of his story, accompanying him in his quest for healing.

The morning brought a sense of urgency as we prepared to transfer him to a better-equipped hospital. Every detail was carefully planned, from arranging the ambulance to ensuring his comfort during the journey. Despite the challenges ahead, my father seemed more confident, ready to face them head-on.

I pledged our enduring support to him, vowing to be by his side every step of the way. His trust in us was evident, fortifying our unbreakable bond.

As we gently transferred him from his bed, each movement executed with utmost care, I found myself in awe of his enduring resilience. Despite the precariousness of his condition, the seamless transition spoke volumes of the dedication of the team.

Inside the ambulance, my uncle's support comforted me. I drove behind the ambulance, listening to the siren. Before, it always made me scared, but now it felt hopeful like it was leading us to a better time ahead.

As we drove through the city, we arrived at the hospital gate and dad was taken out of the ambulance, I looked at him. His face was lit up by the sunlight, making him look peaceful. He seemed to enjoy the small joys of life at that moment. He wished he could feel the warmth of the sun a little longer. Even though we couldn't make that happen, uncle let him know that he understood his wish and that I heard him.

When we arrived at the hospital, we went straight to the emergency department. It was busy, with doctors and nurses moving quickly. They did tests and checks on my father efficiently, showing how dedicated they were to his care.

During the activity, the nurses' words brought me comfort. They were amazed by my father's strength and spirit. They couldn't believe how well he was holding up despite everything he was going through. They said he was truly fighting for his life every day.

At that moment, I felt a mix of pride and gratitude. I silently agreed with the nurses' assessment, knowing deep down that my father was incredibly strong.

Despite the challenges he faced, he continued to fight with an indomitable force that amazed everyone around him.

The medical team admitted dad to the ICU under the care of their best team, and they kindly asked us to leave, assuring us that we could visit him in the evening. As I approached my father, I told him not to worry, reminding him that everything would be fine and that we had come a long way already. I reminded him of the promise of his birthday celebration at home, expressing my excitement at the thought of being together as a family. My father smiled confidently, expressing his eagerness to join us for the celebration and enjoy good food together. I agreed with him and promised to return to see him in the evening; after completing all the necessary documentation, blood tests, and arrangements, my uncle and I prepared to leave the hospital.

Leaving the hospital was hard, but I knew my father was in good hands. After 24 hours of constant worry and vigilance, my body and mind needed a break. As I headed home, I carried with me memories of my father's courage, knowing that his strength would guide me through whatever challenges lay ahead.

As the clock approached 6:00 PM, I found myself rushing to the hospital, driven by the thought that dad might be eagerly awaiting my arrival. Despite my overwhelming fatigue and restlessness, the urgency to check on him overpowered any sense of weariness. Upon reaching the ICU floor, I made my way to the ICU, where dad was admitted. Stepping into his room, a wave of relief flooded over me as I observed him looking noticeably better than before.

Standing beside his bed, I couldn't contain my curiosity and concern. "How are you feeling here, dad?" I inquired, hoping for a positive response. With unwavering confidence, dad stated, "I am much better here. I feel more confident now." His voice carried a sense of assurance that echoed throughout the room. It was evident that the new hospital's facilities and the attentive care provided by its staff had made a significant impact on dad's well-being.

As I handed dad his favorite snack, a mix of roasted dry fruits, his eyes lit up with delight.

Seeing him happy brought a sense of warmth to my heart, momentarily easing the fatigue that lingered from the day's events. "You must be tired," he remarked, his concern for me is touching. I explained to him that I hadn't been getting much rest, and anyways I don't sleep much now. We shared a brief chuckle over our shared experience of my childhood, particularly the amusing incidents where I would fall into deep, unaware sleep that no one could easily rouse me from. The recollection brought forth a wave of nostalgia, mingled with laughter as we recalled those moments of innocence and wonder. It was a reminder of the passage of time, of how swiftly the years had flown by, transforming those long childhood sleeps into brief moments of rest.

Observing dad's improved cough, I felt an overwhelming sense of relief. His progress was a promising sign, a glimmer of hope amidst the instability that surrounded us. His inquiry about everyone at home brought a smile to my face. I updated him on the presence of mom's sister and cousin, who had arrived that afternoon to lend support and companionship to mom. Dad's relief was noticeable as he chuckled softly, expressing gratitude for their presence.

In that moment of lightheartedness, dad seemed eager to share a memory from the past. His eyes twinkled as he recounted tales of bygone days, transporting us both to a time long forgotten yet deeply cherished.

At that moment, my father began to share stories from his life that had shaped him into the resilient person I admired. One particular story stood out about a time when his integrity and leadership were seriously challenged in the All-India Banking Club. He faced accusations that threatened his reputation, which had been built over many years.

Faced with two choices—accept the allegations or fight for the truth at any cost—he chose to fight. With firm determination and strong support from his family, he defended himself. He admitted any unintentional mistakes while bravely standing against injustice.

"In life, there are times when you have to stand strong and fight for what is right," he said, his voice filled with the conviction of someone who had endured many challenges. "Just as I fought those false accusations and other situations, I will fight this virus with all my strength, supported by my unwavering faith in God's blessings."

As the doctor's appointment approached, hope began to stir within me. I couldn't shake the feeling that tomorrow morning's meeting could mark a turning point—a moment where things might improve, offering new hope and a chance for healing.

As the shadows lengthened and the day drew to a close, I gently asked for his permission to step away, urging him not to skip his meals and reminding him that everyone at home was eagerly waiting for your return. I pledged our support and promised that we would see each other tomorrow morning. With a nod of agreement, he entrusted me with the care of our family at home and insisted that I prioritize my well-being by getting proper rest.

Upon reaching home, my mother, unaware of many details, eagerly sought an update. I assured her that everything was fine, explaining that dad was doing great, showing improvement in his condition, and was now stable. A visible sigh of relief escaped her as she absorbed the news. She insisted that I eat and get proper rest, and her concern was evident in her words and gestures.

As I settled into bed, exhaustion weighed heavily upon me, yet with each whispered plea, I prayed to the divine for favorable reports. As sleep finally embraced me, my heart filled with a mix of hope and certainty that couldn't be swayed.

DAY Nine: Amid chaos and hope

At around 8:30 AM, I woke up feeling a bit more relaxed despite the surrounding chaos. Though it was late, I immediately prayed, following up deep breaths, and sought an update on my father's health. I dialed my brother, who had stayed at the hospital overnight. He shared that dad was fine and happy with the treatment, mentioning that he had been asking about me and his beloved home-brewed tea; I told him I would head to the hospital shortly.

As I move out of bed, I see mom seemed worried, having sensed something was off about dad's condition since his previous hospital stay. My aunt and I tried to lift her spirits, emphasizing the positive signs and improvements in dad's health. To divert her hopelessness, I asked mom to prepare tea for dad, knowing it would give her something comforting to focus on. I then began my day with a mix of hope and apprehension, aware of the scheduled doctor's consultation review at 10:30 AM.

After a while, I arrived at the hospital and found my brother, exhausted, waiting outside the ICU. I urged him to go home and rest, assuring him that I would take over from there. I settled in to wait for a chance to see dad. Just then, a doctor summoned me into a consultation room. I handed the tea to the staff and followed the doctor inside.

In the room, the doctor had all of dad's reports laid out and began asking detailed questions: when did dad first have a fever? What medications did he take initially? Why was his COVID test delayed? And when he was initially hospitalized. As we answered, a stark realization emerged in us—we had been negligent. Initially, we assumed dad's fever was just another commonplace ailment similar to the ones my mom and I had recently experienced. We treated it lightly until it escalated. Dad had been on regular antibiotics, which seemed effective until his symptoms worsened, evolving into breathing difficulties and a persistent dry cough. By that point, it was alarmingly clear something more serious was at play. I felt a wave of guilt felt by me, having been away the week dad fell ill and missing the early signs that led to his hospitalization.

The doctor sternly explained that we had wasted five crucial days when the infection could have been controlled easily. After those days, the infection reached a critical stage. He was awed at dad's courage in coping with such a severe infection. I wish I could change the past, but it was too late. The doctor informed us that the infection had worsened over the last six days, leading to fibrosis. This meant his lungs were struggling to breathe and pump due to internal clots forming during the healing process. Despite this, dad was maintaining good vitals, which was a hopeful sign.

Overwhelmed with guilt and anxiety, I couldn't bear the thought of losing my father. I wanted to cry but held back my tears, hiding my emotions from the world. The doctor asked me to accompany him to see dad. We entered the ICU from the doctor's room, surprising dad, who was sipping his tea.

The doctor approached dad's bed with a kind smile. "So, how are you feeling today?"

Dad's eyes lit up with a spark of excitement. "I'm doing great! I feel like I'm in good hands here."

The doctor nodded encouragingly. "That's wonderful to hear. Keep that positive attitude—it will help with your recovery."

While the doctor checked dad's vitals and reviewed his records, he added, "Everything looks good so far. Just keep following our instructions, and you'll be back on your feet in no time."

My father's unwavering positivity, and the doctor's dedication gave me a glimmer of hope amid the turmoil.

As the doctor left back to his office, I softly asked my dad how he was feeling and what his experience had been like so far. He smiled and said, "I am super fine. Better than yesterday, Nurses ask me ten times a day how I'm doing, which gives me a sense of belonging. I feel positive, and I suggest you stay positive and hopeful, too." His words brought a sense of relief to me.

As we talked, my father began showing concern. "How is your mom managing all this?" he asked. "Suddenly, she has a lot of burdens to shoulder. With someone in the family having COVID, people tend to avoid offering help—society, friends, and even the house help may not come. And she might not be healthy enough to handle everything on her own. Is she getting any help? Is she doing okay? How is she managing things at home?"

His questions brought a lump to my throat as I thought about the strain on mom. She had been trying to stay strong, but the weight of the situation was heavy on her shoulders. With friends and neighbors keeping their distance and the absence of our usual help, she was left to manage everything herself. Though my aunt and cousins did their best to support her, it was clear that the situation was taking its toll.

I built his self-assurance, saying, "She is fine, dad, though her main concern is always your health. She keeps asking me about you. So, you have to get better for everyone in the family. You are our strength."

Hearing this, he smiled, showing a quiet confidence. "Things will go well," he said.

At that moment, His concern for my mother's well-being, despite his critical condition, was an indication of his unselfish nature. His belief in overcoming challenges, his unwavering faith, and his love for us gave me hope and strength. We had to hold on to that hope and stay strong, just as he was doing.

I shared with him how the doctor had praised his positivity and courage, remarking how impressive it was. Dad smiled and said, "Why not? I've survived worse in my life, from major operations to job setbacks and family challenges. This is nothing compared to all that. I got through them, and I will survive this as well. I trust in God. I don't know if God exists, but there is someone higher who works day and night for our well-being." I agreed with him and admired his faith.

I asked dad what he felt like eating for dinner. He said, "Anything, as long as it's important to eat right now. We should follow the necessary steps." He softly requested something with a bit of spice but not too much. I nodded and smiled.

I then encouraged him to do some breathing exercises between his therapy sessions. He agreed, and I told him I would leave for now. As soon as I left the room, I felt unsatisfied with the short visit. I wanted to spend more time with him. I stepped back and looked into his ICU room. There he was, sitting straight on his bed, trying to do breathing exercises and hand movements. My heart melted, and I felt both proud and pitiful for my dad.

I started praying silently, thinking that this man was an example for many. I am reflecting on his remarkable presence in our family. He is the embodiment of positivity, a beacon of light in any situation. Just sitting with him, everything seems normal, and the tense lines on my forehead start to fade away. His infectious laughter, his endearing childish nature, and his blend of wisdom and love have a way of making all worries disappear.

I recalled the many phone calls I had with him while I was in Germany, especially on those days when I felt frustrated and overwhelmed. His voice would instantly calm me. "Everything has a solution," he would say. "Nothing is permanent; nothing is too big to take stress over. Live your life happily and make the best out of it." His words were a lifeline, a reminder to keep perspective and find joy even in difficult times.

His advice and encouragement have been my guiding stars, and in moments like these, I realize how deeply I want to live by his wisdom for the rest of my life. As I was lost in thought, dad looked at me, smiled, and we both waved at each other. I gestured that I would see him again later, and he gave me a thumbs-up.

With teary eyes, I left the hospital, the weight of the day pressing heavily on me. As I reached home, the family gathered, eagerly awaiting an update from the doctor's meeting. Although my brother had already informed everyone about dad's latest improvement, they still looked to me for confirmation. I couldn't bring myself to repeat the doctor's detailed analysis, not wanting to break hearts or amplify the guilt over our past negligence. Instead, I simply said that the infection was critical and that his recovery would take longer than usual.

Once things settled down in the living room, I went to my mom and hugged her tightly. "How are you holding up?" I asked gently, sensing her mental state. I shared that dad was concerned about her and had asked about her well-being. She seemed excited to hear more, so I recounted our conversation at the hospital. Mom, who was feeling better now, expressed her plan to visit dad in the evening. I agreed, knowing it would lift both their spirits.

Then she asked the question that made my heart skip a beat: "Will Dad survive this COVID?" The tension in her eyes mirrored my own, bringing a wave of unease, It was a question I was still grappling with myself. After a pause, I looked at her and said, "Trust the process, Mom. He will survive this. He has to. Why are you even questioning it? Yes, the healing will take time, but he will be fine." My words seemed to bring her some comfort, and she took a deep sigh of relief, holding on to the hope that had kept us all going.

In the evening, my family decided to arrange a prayer at the temple, seeking strength and positivity for my dad's speedy recovery. Our faith had been shaken, and turning to God felt like the only way to restore it. Family members, both in the city and beyond, joined in, each praying for dad's recovery in their way.

Later, my mom visited dad. When she returned, she seemed more at peace and comforted by the visit. Seeing her like that brought a sense of calm to all of us. The day had been long and emotionally draining, but it ended with a sense of clarity. We had found answers, determined future actions, and held onto a hopeful outlook.

Mom and Dad enjoying there vacation in manali

DAY Ten: Living in the Present

At 7:00 AM on a foggy winter morning, I woke up with my mind racing, full of worries and uneasiness. Despite starting my day with morning prayers, I stayed on edge. Questions swirled around my head: What if I fail in life? What if things become worse? The more I pondered these thoughts, the more exhausted and drained I felt.

Determined to stay positive, I reminded myself that I am the daughter of a lion. I won't break so easily. I recalled many incidents and teachings from my dad, and each moment spent with him was a valuable lesson. Drawing strength from these memories, I left the bed, feeling a bit more grounded.

After freshening up, I decided to do some breathing exercises to calm my mind. I needed to think clearly during these trying times. I spent about twenty minutes focusing on my breath, trying to gather my thoughts and find a sense of peace. This practice helped me center myself, bringing a small but significant sense of calm amid the storm.

Just as I was beginning to feel a bit more centered, my phone rang at 7:30 AM. It was my brother, who was also constantly worried about dad's situation and often unable to sleep during his hospital shifts. We had arranged for both of my brothers to switch between alternate night shifts, but the stress was still apparent. As we discussed dad's actual condition, our shared concern became evident. We talked about what steps we should take next and ultimately decided to have patience with the treatment, hoping that we might soon see signs of recovery.

My cousin urged me to relax a bit amidst all the hustle, mentioning Dad's C-PAP therapy, which was helping clear his airways by pushing oxygen into his lungs. He assured me that everything would be fine, his words delivering a much-needed sense of certainty. Despite the pervasive worry and doubts, his call helped ease my mind, reminding me that we were all in this together, supporting each other and dad through every step of his recovery.

Today, like every other day, was about staying strong and keeping hope alive, no matter how difficult it seemed.

My mom approached me, concern etched on her face, and asked, "Will you go to the hospital today?" I nodded, replying, "Yes, I am already planning to go." She gently rubbed her hand over my head and said, "You are doing so much for your dad. I pray for your long life and many blessings." Her words, filled with love and tenderness, pierced through my composure. Until that moment, I had managed to stay strong, but her kindness broke through my defenses, and I began to sob uncontrollably.

Seeing my distress, my aunt and brother rushed over, wrapping me in their arms. They offered words of comfort and encouragement. "We are all here for you and are proud of you," my aunt said softly. "You are strong;

don't break like this."

Between my sobs, I managed to voice the worries that had been consuming me. "I don't want to lose my dad. I feel so scared and powerless. I want to do so much to take all his pain away. I can't bear to see him lying on that hospital bed, so exposed, when he has always been so independent and strong."

The words poured out, a torrent of raw emotion. "All I hope for is his life, as he has always embraced it with such happiness and vigor. There is still so much to learn from him. I want to live my dreams with him by my side. Life has to be just with him; he deserves that chance."

At that moment, everyone around me was in tears, sharing in my pain and distress. Though no words could truly comfort me, I felt the collective resilience of their prayers and support. The room was filled with a profound sense of shared emotion, a bond reinforced by our collective love for him.

In a moment of crisis, the words of my mother, aunt, and brother rang like a chorus of strength and support. They reminded me of the sturdiness that runs through my veins, inherited from my strong father. With their encouragement, I gathered my resolve, acknowledging their presence with heartfelt gratitude before splashing cold water on my face to steel myself for the challenge ahead. Holding my father's tea, a familiar comfort in mystification times, I made my way to the hospital.

Approaching my father's room, I took a deep breath, summoning courage from within, and turned the doorknob. Stepping into the room, I was met with my father's warm gaze, filled with relief and longing. His simple question, "Where were you? I was waiting for you," was loaded with emotion, proof of his desire for my presence in his time of need.

"Dad, I got late today because I had to give my helping hands at home," I replied. He mentioned feeling a bit weak; I immediately started checking his daily reports, which had become a ritual. While I was going through the reports, dad asked, "What's there in my report? Is everything okay? I've heard that with COVID, your organs can start getting weak and might collapse."

His words scared me, but I kept my focus on the reports. I saw that all his results were fine, except for the significant drop in his oxygen levels. The increased CO_2 ratio was a major concern. I closed the file and approached him to calm his nerves.

"Dad, everything is fine. Look at these parameters," I said, showing him the report. "Every single thing is within range. Your vitals are good, and your blood pressure is fine. You will win this race for life." I smiled, feeling a sense of relief.

Dad nodded and said, "Yes, I will trust the process." Then, he began expressing concern about the money we were spending on his health. As a professional bank financial manager, he wanted to inquire about the expenses related to the hospital and medicines.

"Dad," I replied, "you shouldn't be focusing on these things now. Don't waste your precious energy and oxygen, your health is more valuable than money," I added in a humorous and teasing way. "There are already people to think about all this. Everything else can be managed, but your life and time are priceless. So, don't worry about anything and just focus on getting better." He smiled back and agreed.

I rubbed his hand and gently massaged his head for a while, offering him some comfort. As he began to feel sleepy, I stood by his side, silently watching over him. After a moment, I decided it was time to leave, but not before promising him that I would return in the evening. He nodded in agreement, a small smile playing on his lips.

Leaving the hospital, I knew we had to keep going, drawing strength and hoping for a better tomorrow. After reaching home, I completed the pending chores that needed attention and took some hours of sleep.

It was 5:30 PM when I woke up, finding my mom already prepared to head to the hospital for her evening visit. "Are you going alone?" I asked. She nodded, saying, "Yes, you need proper rest, so I'll go with my brother." But I insisted, "No, I will accompany you."

As we discussed our plans, my brother chimed in, sharing a touchingly humorous detail. "Dad is refusing to eat anything without me there, suggesting that I call my daughter. She has a special talent for making me eat properly." We chuckled at the thought, planning to discuss it with dad.

A few minutes later, I accompanied my mom to the hospital. As we approached the ICU, dad's face lit up with happiness at the sight of us; after my mom's long visit with my dad in the ICU, I quickly wanted to check on him. Upon entering the room, dad and I began to share updates about our day. Dad inquired about the health of his brother, too, to which I gave him assurance, "Everyone is fine, taking proper medications and precautions." I could sense his longing for his brother's presence.

I remembered a time not long ago when dad talked about how beautiful the Northern Lights were and how he wanted to visit Europe again to see them. I asked, "dad, is your Northern Lights plan still on?"

He replied, "Yes, that's beautiful, but I don't know if I can go there now."

"Why not?" I said, trying to encourage him. "You enjoy life to the fullest, traveling and exploring the world," He replied. No, I will plan that with you," I insisted. He smiled at my determination.

After a moment, he said, "We are humans; we don't know everything. I've lived my life to the best, in good and bad times. That's what I want to give you—a life full of learning from my experiences. I don't have many wishes left."

He continued, "I don't plan for years. All I have is now. I've always tried to adapt to life's situations, and I've done that my whole life. The gifts people give, even if they're expensive, aren't as meaningful as living in the moment. This reminds me of the times when my mom and I used to tell him not to wear newly gifted shirts right away to save them for special occasions and to use less perfume so it wouldn't run out quickly. He always replied that when the time came, he would buy new ones. We often argued about it, but looking back, I realize dad was always right about living in the present."

As he spoke, I felt a mix of emotions—gratitude for his wisdom, sadness for his weakened state, and hope that we could still make those dreams come true. His words reminded me of the depth of his understanding and the richness of his experiences, which he had always generously shared with us.

Our discussion was interrupted several times by the nurse, reminding me that visiting hours were over. "Dad, I have to leave now," I said gently, "but I promise I'll be back tomorrow early morning. I'm hoping for an even better visit then." I hold his hand, wanting to convey my commitment and hope for his recovery.

As I left the hospital, my heart was heavy but also filled with admiration for my father's wisdom and strength. He had always lived in the moment, adapting to life's challenges with grace. On the way home, my mom and I shared our experiences from the visit with dad, which were filled with positivity and learning.

Back home, I felt the weight of the day's emotions. I had dinner with the whole family. As I drifted off to sleep, I prayed for dad's recovery and the hope that tomorrow would bring better news ahead.

DAY Eleven: Unwavering Faith: Trusting the Experts

At 7:00 AM, the morning started with a jolt, the sharp ring of my brother's phone shattering the fragile peace in the house. I woke up to the sound of urgent discussions and raised voices. "What happened?" I asked, still groggy. My aunt replied, "It was a call from the hospital. They need dad's clothes." I asked, "For what?" but her silence spoke volumes.

Tension filled the room as everyone began speculating, each theory more frightening than the last. My heart pounded in sync with the growing panic. My mother, already fragile in both heart and hope, was hit hardest by this morning's request. Her sister stood by her side, trying to offer comfort. I watched my mom from a distance, feeling helpless and unsure of what to say. Consoling wasn't my strong suit, especially when I was grappling with my fears.

My brother, who was already at the hospital, called again, urging us to hurry. I asked him the reason, and he said, "I don't know much, but the nurse said he had excessive sweat, and dad wanted to wear his clothes from home." Excessive sweating? Out of what? No one could give a clear answer, so we rushed to the hospital, my mind swirling with a hundred dreadful possibilities.

Halfway there, another call from my brother came through. "He's fine," which was a sense of big relief. "Don't panic. They've already changed his clothes." His words offered a small but significant relief, calming some of the worry that had gripped us all.

As we arrived at the hospital, I felt a knot tighten in my stomach. I was nervous to see my dad, apprehensive of what I might find. But I needed to see him myself to be sure he was okay. Gathering all my courage, I walked into the ICU room. He was there, sitting on his bed, looking tired but calm. Seeing him like that, my unease began to fade, replaced by a deep sense of care.

I stepped closer, and at that moment, I realized how much resolve it takes to face our deepest concerns sometimes and how vital it is to hold onto hope, even when things seem unpredictable.

As I approached his bed, I could see that Dad wanted to share a lot with me. There was a look in his eyes—a mixture of hope and disarray, as if he had been waiting for us. His face brightened slightly when I came closer and gently held his shoulder. Despite his frailty, there was a determination in his gaze, a silent reinforcement.

"Is everything ok? Dad," I asked gently.

"I don't know," he replied, his voice tinged with confusion. "I get so much sweat in my body that I wake up wet. They checked everything about my heart, but it seems everything is fine. Did you make sure from a doctor?" He looked at me, his eyes betraying a hint of unease about his condition.

"Not yet," I admitted. "I wanted to check on you first."

He nodded and continued. "At home, you all must have been a bit scared, right?"

Everyone cares about you and prays for your well-being day and night. We are all looking forward to the time when the family can get together, something everyone is eagerly waiting for. We can spend the whole night laughing over silly talks for no reason. I am hopeful that this time will come soon; just this situation needs to pass quickly.

"It's good to know they're there," he said softly, a small smile forming on his lips. "I was worried about you all."

I nodded, feeling a wave of emotions. "We're managing everything at home, dad. We just want you to get better."

As I stood there, the situation he faced earlier this morning replayed in my mind, causing me to feel overwhelmed. As my hopes were shaking, and I kept thinking about what I could do and what decisions we should make as a family. I couldn't stop myself from asking my dad questions: "What were you feeling when you started sweating? How are you feeling now?

Should we consider changing the hospital or doctor? Have they done any tests yet?"

My dad looked at me, noticing my shaken confidence with my questions. I had always been strong in front of him, but in that moment, I was faltering. He gently asked, "Why are you panicking? I'm okay. First, If you do things while panicking, most of the time, you'll do them wrong. You need to hold yourself together. Discuss everything with uncle and everyone at home. More importantly, don't make any decisions until you meet the doctor and ask him all your doubts. Try to understand what he has to say. Also, remember that we shouldn't try to be the best in every area of life or make all the right decisions; we should trust those who are experts in their fields. The world runs on trust, and it always will. God has created everyone uniquely in their own way, so trust the creation. The right decisions are always made when you are in the right frame of mind, not being impulsive. Relax, and yes, I am perfectly fine. The doctor might come in sometime, so ask outside about his appointments and meet him first."

As he spoke, his wisdom began to calm the cascade of fears in my mind, bringing me back to a sense of reality and trust. I listened, and for a few seconds, I stood silent beside him. He noticed and tried to divert the situation, "What is the schedule for physiotherapy today? Do you know? I will find out, dad, I said softly. Tell at home that dad is fine now. He added there's no need to worry about what happened; it may just be a situation and nothing more. Find a solution comprehensively. Sit with everyone, relax, and plan things following up on the appointment. Follow the process and leave the rest to God. Everything is destined, and it's always for the good."

I held my dad's hand and looked at the cannula placed in it. His hand had turned blue and swollen from the continuous drips and medicines. I rubbed it softly and asked, "Does it hurt?"

"Not usually," he replied, "But the ABG test hurts, which is used to check oxygen levels. But I'm stronger than you know." He added a smile.

Absorbing his wisdom, I didn't want to leave him. Then, the nurse called at the end of the visit and requested that I leave the ICU. I told dad, "I'll come back soon. I'll see things through and discuss with everyone."

Outside the ICU, I asked the receptionist about the doctor's appointment. She told me the doctor had already arrived and asked me to wait for about fifteen minutes. Sitting outside his office, I felt nervous, with my legs shaking and a knot of terror in my stomach. To distract myself, I thought about what my dad had said and started thinking about my life. I realized I had often made quick decisions when I was angry, stressed, or anxious and later regretted them. This was a moment for me to learn and change my approach, to handle situations calmly and wisely, knowing there are always choices in every situation.

As I was lost in my thoughts, the doctor arrived and called me into his room. I went and sat across from the doctor. There was a short pause before I gathered the courage to ask, "Do you have any update on dad? He had excessive sweating excessively today. What's the reason for it? Is it related to his heart?" The idea of a heart problem was the first thing that came to my mind.

The doctor said, "The sweating isn't anything serious. It might be from a bad dream or extreme anxiety. We've done tests and are keeping an eye on his heart, and everything looks fine there.

But there's something important I need to tell you." My heart raced, and I felt a sudden wave of panic.

He went on, "Our bodies have a natural healing process, like when we form clots after an injury. Lungs, which expand and contract to pump oxygen, usually heal by themselves. But because of his low immunity, age, and past smoking, his fibrosis condition hasn't improved."

I was overwhelmed by this information, unsure how to react. I asked the obvious question, "What's the solution to this now?"

The doctor said, "Fibrosis cannot be completely cured. There's no known cure for it yet.

However, since his other organs are working well, they will compensate for the lungs over time. It's a slow healing process that requires patience and long-term care. I can recommend one of the top pulmonologists in India who specializes in post-COVID cases and lung functions. He taught me during my training, and I keep in touch with him. I've discussed your case with him and shared your reports. It would be beneficial for you to meet him in person. He may suggest a different approach based on your current situation."

He called the specialist and requested an appointment. The specialist agreed to see us and suggested that two family members come to visit Delhi to discuss the case. This specialist also emphasized the importance of physiotherapy, reminding me of my dad's inquiries about the sessions back in the ICU.

I left the room with a clearer understanding of my dad's condition, knowing that his fibrosis was critical. As I was leaving, the doctor called me back. "You can bring your father home in a few days if you want; this healing journey takes time. We recommend setting up an ICU at home with all necessary equipment and a full-time nurse. I can help arrange everything. Being at home surrounded by family and having home-cooked food will make your father happier and aid in his recovery. But first, try to meet the specialist in Delhi."

I noted everything the doctor said and left the room with a sense of purpose. Dad would love this news, and it would double his courage. I inquired about the session at the reception and found out it was scheduled for an hour later. I wouldn't be able to see dad for a few hours, but I felt slightly relieved knowing that the morning's condition wasn't serious and that dad might soon come home, which would make everyone happy and relieved.

On my way out, I picked up the necessary medicines for him and headed home. The thought of dad being in a familiar environment, surrounded by family and comforted by home-cooked meals, lifted my spirits. It felt like a positive step forward.

As I reached home, I felt a mix of relief and anticipation, ready to share the hopeful update with my family; I saw the worried faces of my family members, especially my mom. Even though I had been conveyed over the phone, the tension was unmistakable. I knew I had to keep my composure.

I sat down with everyone, feeling it was necessary to help them understand the situation better without adding unnecessary stress. I didn't want to share everything the doctor had told me, as it would only add to their worry. Instead, I assured them what happened today was not serious. I explained that the doctor suggested dad could come home soon since the treatment process is long and that we could also arrange an ICU setup at home. This news visibly relieved my mom, who immediately started discussing how we would set everything up. My uncle chimed in, offering to arrange oxygen cylinders and other necessary equipment through his contacts.

These family moments are a healing therapy for me. Seeing everyone working together and doing their best for dad and each other was comforting. My uncle, who has now recovered from COVID-19, offered to go meet the specialist doctor in Delhi. However, after a while, he suggested it would be best if I went. He believed I needed to get all my questions answered by the specialist and see everything for myself while he managed things with dad here. I agreed and decided to go with my brother the next day. While everyone at home started arranging things, I rested after having tea with them.

At 5:00 PM, I got a call from my brother. He told me dad was asking about me. He said he had visited him twice, and dad is fine now and had nothing to worry about, but he hadn't eaten anything, so I should come during the evening visiting time. After an hour I gathered some tofu and his favorite snacks that mom had prepared and headed to the hospital.

As I arrived at the hospital, I saw my brother in the hallway. He shared an incredible story about dad's bravery. Earlier, while he was inside the room, the doctor came to start Dad's C-PAP therapy. During the mask change, there was a longer gap without oxygen, causing dad's levels to drop significantly. Despite this, dad remained calm and composed. The doctor immediately scolded the staff for the delay, but dad, showing remarkable courage, surprised everyone by saying, "It's okay, it happens. I am fine." Hearing this, I was both amused and deeply moved by dad's strength and agreed with my brother's admiration.

With a mixture of awe and concern, I moved to dad's ICU room. As I entered, I saw him already looking at the clock, clearly waiting for me. As soon as he saw me, he said, "Where were you? I was looking at the time and thinking you said you'd come in sometime, but it's almost late evening." His words carried a blend of worry and relief. I walked over to him with a warm smile, apologizing for the delay and assuring him I was here now. I then offered him the tofu and his favorite snacks that mom had prepared, hoping to bring him some comfort and joy.

"Dad, why haven't you eaten anything? I don't like it," I said with concern.

He replied, "I don't feel like eating."

Firmly, I responded, "But you have to. There's no other choice for you."

"Yes, okay, but I'm tired of almost the same food, and there's no spice. Since I haven't moved all day, how will the old food digest?" he said humorously.

"Dad, don't make excuses. We can ask for different food if possible, but you can't refuse to eat," I said, smiling yet firmly.

Wanting to lift his spirits, I shared some positive news from the doctor. "The doctor said you can come home soon." His face lit up with a smile I hadn't seen in a long time.

Dad trying to put me at ease, "There was nothing serious today, whatever happened." I nodded, "I know, dad. I had a meeting with the doctor. You are the bravest person I know, not just because you're my father, but because I truly admire you. The audacity you showed today was a true example of resolve. You will recover soon." His eyes sparkled with hope and gratitude.

"Yes, why not? I will recover. Being around you all makes me happy, and everything I eat will work twice as well," he said with determination. I agreed and shared how the doctor had praised his willpower. Dad smiled and said, "This is just another one. With all of your support, I will get through it."

Just then, the doctor came in and advised me to add more natural proteins to dad's diet, despite the hospital's protein supplements. He asked if dad was a non-vegetarian and ate meat. When I told him dad is vegetarian, the doctor suggested trying chicken soup, as it could be beneficial.

Dad, watching our conversation and trying to read our lips, asked later what we were discussing. I told him, "Nothing serious. The doctor just wants us to give you more protein, and he suggested you eat non-veg." Soon, dad made a face, and we shared a light moment, laughing about it. His laughter turned into a cough, and I quickly rubbed his back, asking him to relax.

Emotionally, it was a rollercoaster of a day, but seeing my family and dad happy brought me a sense of peace. I realized that sometimes it's best to keep certain things to yourself and only share what is helpful for the situation. As the day drew to a close, I left the hospital with a whirlwind of thoughts, but also with renewed strength from seeing everyone in good spirits. I prayed for everyone struggling in life and for my entire family. Feeling grateful, I finally drifted off to sleep.

DAY Twelve: Nostalgic Reflections

At 5:30 AM, the doorbell rang. As a light sleeper, I woke up immediately, my heart racing. Who could be outside on this freezing winter morning? Sometimes, everything feels more intense and negative at such early hours. I rushed to the gate but saw no one. Just as I was about to return inside, I heard someone call my name. I turned around to see my neighbor standing a distance away, wearing a mask and clearly wary of COVID-19. He asked for an update about Dad, then revealed the real reason for his visit: "Could you park your car sideways? It's causing problems with parking." I agreed and moved the car. When I returned to bed, I found myself bit restless.

I slept for a while before my phone rang. It was my brother calling from the hospital. "Dad is asking about you," he said. "Will you bring him some tea?"

"Yes, I'll come in a bit. How is he now? How are his oxygen levels and vitals?" I replied.

"They're usually okay," he answered, "but there have been some fluctuations. And yesterday, he unexpectedly refused to continue his physiotherapy session after a while, even though he was the one who asked for it."

I felt a twinge of concern. "Why did he refuse it?" I wondered aloud. "I'll come over soon."

After hanging up, I got out of bed, my thoughts racing. It was confusing and worrying that Dad had refused the therapy when he had been so eager about it the day before. I needed to get to the hospital quickly, not just to bring him tea but to understand what was going on.

As I brewed some tea, adding a bit of ginger the way Dad liked it, my mom woke up and came into the kitchen. "It's so early. Are you going to the hospital?" she asked.

"Yes, Mom. Dad is asking for some homemade tea," I replied.

She came closer, hugged me, kissed my forehead, and wished me all the happiness and success in our efforts for Dad. With teary eyes, I hugged her back, and we both began reminiscing about the days when we were all together, teasing each other, enjoying little moments, and laughing out loud.

Mom started sharing memories of Dad, even when he had a light cold. He would make faces and pretend to be seriously ill just to gather everyone around him and talk. Now, despite knowing how serious his condition is, he shows so much courage and endurance, still trying to keep everyone positive and hopeful.

I agreed with her and recalled those small incidents. "This is his real power," I said. "He knows how to handle situations and turn things around."

We both sipped our tea while sharing stories from the past and planning for the home ICU setup. Afterward, I packed the tea and snacks and left for the hospital.

As I reached the hospital, I found my brother in the hallway outside dad's room. "How is he now?" I asked.

"He still has those oxygen-level fluctuations, even when he tries to sit and talk more," my brother said. My mind was filled with concern.

I walked into the ICU. His face lit up when he saw me. "Here's your tea, dad," I said, handing him the cup.

"Thank you," he replied, taking a sip. "I've been waiting for you."

"I heard you refused your physiotherapy session yesterday," I said gently. "What happened?"

He sighed, looking a bit guilty. "I was tired. It felt too much for me."

I nodded, trying to understand. "But you asked about it yesterday. You were so eager."

"I know," he admitted. "But when the time came, I just couldn't do it. It was harder than I thought."

I sat down beside him, holding his hand. "It's okay, dad. We'll take it one step at a time. You can go at your pace."

He squeezed my hand. "Yes, I want to get better, but sometimes it's overwhelming."

"I understand," I assured him. "We're all here to support you. And remember, you'll be coming home soon. We're setting everything up for you."

His face softened with a small smile. "Home sounds good."

While talking to dad, I placed my hand on his shoulder and started rubbing it gently. His shoulder bones were more pronounced than before, a stark reminder of how weak and thin he had become. The sight pained me deeply.

To assist him with eating and drinking, I switched his mask to a nasal cannula, which I had become familiar with handling. During the switch, I observed a drop in his blood-oxygen level while he was using the nasal cannula. It briefly fell to 58, which immediately alarmed me. Typically, levels would momentarily drop and then stabilize once the nasal cannula was properly adjusted. However, this time, his blood-oxygen saturation lingered at a critically low 70-72, even with the supply set to high.

Dad started to panic, gasping for air. Seeing him struggle like this made my legs shake, and my hands freeze. The nurse, who had been observing, quickly came over to check on him. He examined dad's breathing pattern and said, "No, put back the normal mask. He can't maintain proper oxygen levels with the nasal cannula right now."

I held dad's hand tightly as we switched back the mask. His face was turning red, and he was gasping for oxygen. I felt numb, unable to comprehend what was happening. His condition seemed to be worsening, and there was little I could do at that moment. After a few tense moments, dad's breathing stabilized. I asked him to take deep breaths while I held his hand, urging him to rest and avoid talking too much for the moment.

I thought about my pollen allergies and how suffocating they could be. When I had an allergy attack, I struggled with suffocation and chest congestion. Proper oxygen flow was critical. I couldn't imagine how dad was managing day after day in a constant state of breathlessness. His endurance was incredible.

"Dad, you need to eat something," I said softly, but he shook his head.

"No, I don't want to eat," he replied quickly, his nervousness evident.

"Dad, you are stronger than I ever knew," I said. He is still trying to manage proper oxygen flow with deep breaths.

"That's why I want my family around. You were here this time, but I'm scared of what might happen when no one is here," he confessed, his voice trembling.

"Don't think about that now. Just rest. Your blood-oxygen levels are fine," I reassured him. I carefully removed his mask briefly to give him a few sips of tea and then provided the protein shakes from the nurse. "Everything will be fine." Since he was stable, I promised to return in a few hours to check on him. He agreed, and I suggested he try to sleep or rest without overthinking.

As I left the ICU, my heart was heavy with worry. Seeing dad in such a state was incredibly hard. But amidst the struggle, there were small moments of hope. Each day is a battle; I prayed silently for his recovery and the well-being of everyone struggling with their battles in life.

When I arrived home, everyone looked to me for an update on the visit. I briefed everyone on dad's condition, which was limited in detail, and soon, we all began planning for what lay ahead. We divided the responsibilities: my uncle continued arranging the oxygen cylinders while my mom and I focused on setting up the home ICU. The rest of the day was a blur of phone calls, planning, and coordination.

By evening, we had made significant progress. The specialist appointment was scheduled after 2 days, which we are trying to postpone if possible, and the home setup was nearly complete. As I sat down for a moment of rest, I felt a mix of exhaustion and hope. Seeing dad smile today had been a small victory, and it gave me the strength to keep going.

At 6:00 PM, it was time for my visit to the ICU. Despite feeling a bit scared as I approached the hospital,

I pushed through my exhaustion with a steadfast determination to see dad. As I arrived at the ICU, I spotted the doctor standing outside his room. He noticed me and came over, placing a supporting hand on my shoulder.

"Keep it up, dear," he said, his voice gentle. He then placed his hand on my head. "Why are you so worried? You're doing the best you can, and that's all anyone can ask. Take some rest for yourself and relax. Let your dad rest as well. I can see you all are worried about him, but we're doing everything we can to discharge him to go home soon. We're monitoring him closely. His oxygen levels are fluctuating a bit, so we did a few tests—an X-ray and D-dimer—to ensure there's no blood clotting in his body. I've already instructed the nurse for reports, so try to worry less and relax. Meet him and encourage him to be patient."

My throat choked up, and tears began to well up in my eyes, though I tried to mask my emotions. The doctor noticed and consoled me. In a heavy voice, I asked, "Will he be fine?"

"We are trying our best and hoping for a positive outcome," the doctor replied. He added after looking at dad's report, "His other tests are fine, which is a good sign, but his D-dimer levels are higher than we'd like. This is concerning because of his past heart history, but we're doing everything we can. Remember, God is the ultimate healer."

After saying this, the doctor left, and I entered the ICU. Dad was sleeping, and I didn't want to wake him. As I approached and looked over his daily routine updates file, he stirred and woke up. Seeing me, he nodded slightly and asked if everything was alright.

"Yes, everything is fine," I encouraged him, trying to keep my voice steady. "While you were sleeping, I was just looking at your updates. Why haven't you eaten anything other than protein shakes?"

"I don't feel like eating," he replied.

I had brought some tofu pieces with me, dad. He immediately declined, saying he didn't want to eat. The nurse mentioned that he had refused to eat anything since morning because he was scared of removing his oxygen mask.

"No, dad, you have to eat. It's really important for you, and you can't go without eating anything," I told him firmly.

After some persuasion, he agreed, and I started giving him one piece at a time. Slowly, he began eating, gaining confidence with each bite. Watching him eat, even just a little, brought a wave of relief. We had found a way for him to eat without hesitation, at least for now.

As he ate, I continued to uplift his spirit. "Everyone at home is eager to see you and spend time with you. We are arranging everything so you can be comfortable. Just keep your will strong, as you always have."

He nodded, Bit confused, but there was a flicker of hope in his eyes. I knew it was crucial to keep his spirits up and his will strong. Every small victory, like getting him to eat, was a step forward in this long journey.

After dad finished eating, he asked me a question that caught me completely off guard. "Can you help me write a book?"

At this moment, amidst the stress and worry, it seemed like an odd request. "Yes, of course. Why now? How did this question come to your mind at this moment? And what exactly do you want to write about?"

Dad, deep in thought, replied, "About my dad. He was my biggest inspiration in life. I learned so much from him. He was my strength until he lived, and he always guided me through thick and thin. As long as he was around, I lived carefree, knowing he had my back. He got me out of many difficult situations in life. He was always calm, composed, and solution-oriented.

My grandfather, as much as I know about him, was exactly like that. He inspired many in our family and among his friends. I heard his stories and spent some childhood time with him."

I agreed wholeheartedly. "Yes, I will help you write it. You can share your thoughts, and I'll help put them into words."

He nodded, a spark of determination in his eyes. "Once I am out of all this, that's what I'm going to do."

I alleviated him, "Yes, of course."

Dad continued, briefly sharing how his father's sudden demise broke him and forced him to become mature overnight. "He left me pretty soon. Sometimes, I regret that I could have learned a lot more from him while he was still here. But I still think of him in any situation in life. He is my guide, even now."

I realized how every father is indeed the first teacher and a lifelong inspiration for their child. "You're not alone, dad. Everyone is worried about you at home most of the time. And in the hospital, someone from the family or I will always be with you. If you need anything, just ask the nurse."

The nurse came for a visit, "This guy really takes care of me. He makes me comfortable; he's a really nice guy." Turning to the nurse, he introduced me, "She is my daughter. She lives and works in Germany."

We had a short conversation, and the nurse assured me, "Don't worry about him. He is our responsibility here."

I told dad, "If you need anything, we are right outside. Just rest now, and I will come back in some time."

He seemed curious about who had come to visit him or who might be visiting soon. With a longing in his eyes, he mentioned my uncle and aunt, who live in Rajasthan. "I miss them," he said softly. "When will they come?"

Seeing the emotion on his face, I gently updated him, "They want to meet you too, dad. They will be here in a day or two."

He sighed with relief, a hint of a smile touching his lips. "Okay," he said, his voice a bit lighter. It was clear that the thought of seeing them brought him some comfort.

After a while, I exited the room; I saw dad's best friend sitting outside, waiting to meet dad, though visiting hours were already over. The nurse returned and said they needed some medicines, so I asked my brother to get them while I chatted with dad's childhood friend. He shared some wonderful memories from their time together. He talked about how my dad had always been the leader of their group despite not being very tall. His courage and confidence made him stand out. They were a tight-knit group of friends in college, always ready to take on any challenge. They were quite popular, and he recounted tales of their escapades.

One story, in particular, stood out. They had helped one of their friends elope. They all boarded a train to leave the city, and when people came searching for them, they jumped off the moving train to escape. It sounded like something straight out of a movie. As he recounted this adventure, I burst into laughter, momentarily forgetting the heavy weight of worry. The laughter brought a sense of lightness and relief, a welcome break from the tension of the past days.

Soon, my brother returned and told me to give him medicines in the ICU as dad would be happy to see me. When I re-entered the room, dad was both shocked and delighted to see me again.

"Uncle has come to meet you," I said, and he became excited, insisting that we let him in for some time.

Soon, I stepped out to convey this, but his friend had already left. Not wanting to disappoint dad, I called his childhood friend. "Where are you, uncle? Dad wants to see you."

"I'll be there in five minutes," he replied.

I knew this visit would make dad very happy. Once I knew his friend was on his way, I left the hospital, feeling a bit lighter despite the late hour. I needed rest, but the thought of dad smiling when he saw his friend gave me a sense of peace I hadn't felt in days.

I had dinner with my family at home and shared the stories dad's friends had told during their visit. As I recounted the tales of their college days and their daring adventures, we all laughed, reminiscing about similar stories from the past. Despite the tiredness from the day's events, the evening ended on a nostalgic note.

We relived old memories and reflected on the unique impact and importance of every relationship in life. Each story reminded us of how these connections shape our lives in different ways. We expressed our heartfelt wishes and prayers for dad's speedy recovery, hoping to create many more cherished memories with him in the future.

The evening was a beautiful reminder of the strength and joy that come from each bond and shared experience in life.

DAY Thirteen: The Story Behind the Book Title

At 7:00 AM, while I was still half asleep, I heard voices, hushes, and discussions between my mom and aunt. They were talking about setting up a home ICU, eating rich protein foods, and giving dad lots of coconut water throughout the day. My thoughts swung between sleep, their voices, and concerns about dad's health. Soon, my mom came to me and gently woke me up, saying, "dad must be waiting for you."

"Yes," I replied, quickly getting up. "What's the update on meeting with the pulmonologist in Delhi?" I asked.

She sighed softly and said, "He's in Mumbai doing some research and an emergency, so he can only meet us tomorrow."

As I processed this information, A flood of mixed emotions engulfed me. The urgency of our situation, the hope for expert advice, and the constant worry about dad's condition weighed heavily on my mind. The day's activities loomed large, but the thought of dad's recovery kept me going.

Mom handed me a cup of tea as I woke up. Sitting on my bed, I sought a moment of respite and a bit of energy. As we all sipped our tea together, we discussed our plans for a home care nurse. Mom was particularly excited about the idea of body massages to help dad regain his strength. Her enthusiasm brought a mix of emotions to me. Given dad's situation, I wasn't entirely sure if his urgent and emergency needs could be properly managed at home. Despite these concerns, I held on to optimism, hoping that everything would turn out fine.

After a while, I called my brother at the hospital and asked for an update on dad's health. He said, "He is fine. His oxygen levels are stable after being placed on C-PAP therapy several times. He seems fine." Feeling relieved, I asked him to give dad breakfast. My cousin shared that he had already tried, but dad insisted, "Call Naina. She has better practice." Realizing that dad needed me, I assured him I would come soon. As I was freshening up, my mom gave me tea for dad. I got ready and left for the hospital within 15 minutes.

Upon arriving at the hospital, I saw a nurse for home care waiting for me outside the ICU. As I spoke with her, it was clear that she was mature, experienced, and patient. She expressed her willingness to join us at home to help. Grateful for her offer, I finalized the arrangements and told her I would inform her when we were ready for her to start. With that sorted, I quickly moved to the ICU.

As I looked at dad, he seemed uncomfortable with the C-PAP mask as it covered his face completely, preventing him from speaking and making him feel confined. He signaled to me, asking if he could remove it. I insist him, "Just ten more minutes, dad, and then you can remove it to eat something." He showed me a thumbs-up, his eyes filled with gratitude and weariness.

He was trying to share so much through his expressions, but I told him, "Right now, just rest and don't speak much. It takes too much effort to talk." I left the ICU for a few minutes and engaged in a conversation with one of the doctors outside. He shared some insights about COVID cases, emphasizing that recovery often depended on a person's will and immunity. He recounted stories of patients with severe infections who had survived and, after a year, were able to walk and live healthily, albeit with some limitations due to fibrosis.

"The only condition," he said, "is that your dad might not be able to walk fast, climb stairs, or run. His lungs won't allow such activity, and recovery will take time."

I nodded, feeling a ray of hope. "As long as he's with us, time is not a problem. We'll get through this."

The doctor suggested ensuring much care at home and emphasized the importance of a balanced diet to counter the side effects of the heavy medicines dad was taking. It was an informative and optimistic conversation.

With the meeting time running out, I went back inside the ICU. Dad was still lying there, looking at me with hopeful eyes. I made sure he was comfortable, encouraging him to eat and rest.

He looked so emotional, trying to convey so much without words. His hand slowly slipped off the bed, a gesture that filled me with a sense of his hopelessness. I knew he was fighting with all his might, but the long struggle had worn him down. It was only natural for him to sometimes lose hope, and I understood that.

After a brief, heavy silence, I gently asked him how he was feeling. He responded with expressive eyes and slight hand movements, unable to speak much. His expressions spoke volumes: he felt like a burden on us. He saw us constantly panicking and arranging things for him, and he wanted to help but couldn't. This realization triggered emotions within me, but I quickly composed myself, not wanting to appear weak in front of him.

I placed my hand on his head and started gently rubbing it. "Dad," I said softly, "you're thinking too much. Be the strong person you are. This doesn't suit your personality. You are our strength, and you can't lose hope like this. Have patience, and everything will be fine."

He nodded, offering a faint grin to reassure me. He tried to say something, but I couldn't understand him. So, I handed him a notebook from the nearby table, encouraging him to write down his thoughts. With shaking hands, he struggled to form words on the paper. After a few moments, he managed to write: "Yes, I am 100% sure I will come out of this."

Reading his words overwhelmed me with emotions. Despite everything, his courage and determination shone through. Tears welled up in my eyes, but this time, they were tears of pride and inspiration. "Dad," I said, my voice choked with emotion, "I am so proud of you. You are the best."

His eyes softened, and I could see a spark of hope reignite within him. He held my hand gently, a silent promise that he would keep fighting. At that moment, I realized that his strength was not just physical but deeply rooted in his spirit.

There was silence, but it was a comforting silence filled with unspoken words of love and support. I knew the journey ahead could be tough, but with dad's indomitable spirit and our family's unwavering support, we would face it together. The road to recovery might be long, but if we had each other, I was confident we could get through anything.

I requested the nurse to change his mask and put on the normal one. The nurse helped me, and as we were changing the mask, the nurse asked dad how he was feeling. Dad immediately responded, "Yes, I am fine and doing well with all your support and love. Just worried about your struggle which you all are doing for me" I added, "Don't worry dad. Everyone here is doing everything they can without feeling burdened, and that is the best part."

Once dad had his regular mask back on, he seemed so relieved and excited. He felt free and no longer suffocated. I noticed that his oxygen levels were maintained well, staying above ninety. He asked me, "What did you bring for me?"

I replied, "Tofu and boiled egg whites." He looked pleased and eagerly asked for some salt as his taste buds were changing. He also requested sprouts for the later evening, his favorite, which is packed with protein. "If I can eat that, it would help me," he said.

I promised him, "Sure, dad. As we talked, I started giving him one piece of tofu at a time. He chewed slowly, savoring the food, and it was clear that the simple act of eating brought him a small measure of comfort and normalcy."

As he ate, I noticed how frail he had become. His shoulder bones jutted out, and he looked thinner than ever. It pained me to see him like this. Despite the physical weakness, there was a spark in his eyes—a determination to fight and get better.

As I fed him small bites of food, I said, "mom is very excited about you coming home. She has all these plans to help you get better."

Dad smiled weakly, "That sounds nice. I miss home."

After making sure dad was comfortable and had eaten enough, I sat by his side, holding his hand. The nurse came in to check his vitals, and I asked about the tests and his current condition. She assured me that they were monitoring him closely and that the daily report was fine.

Dad now I will leave till then you take care everyone is outside if you need anything, I said.

Dad nodded and said yes, I am fine now. You can go and take care of everyone at home as everyone is already doing a lot.

With that, I left the hospital, and at that moment, I wasn't exactly sure how I was feeling. There was joy at the thought of seeing dad home soon but also concern about his deteriorating condition. I drove home, my thoughts swirling around dad's condition and the plans we were making.

As I reached home, there were similar discussions about dad's condition, how it all started, and how his progress was happening day and night at home. These conversations were emotionally draining, filling me with guilt and frustration about the situation. Often, I found myself moving to another room or engaging in something important to avoid the constant repetition.

After settling at home for a while, I helped mom with some tasks she was managing. My aunt, uncle, and cousins were always around for support, managing things both at home and at the hospital. Their presence was a great comfort, and I appreciated their help immensely.

I took a short rest, planning for the next morning's visit to the pulmonary specialist and researcher. My brothers, noticing my exhaustion, brought me my favorite snacks. Their gesture of care touched me deeply, reminding me that even in this challenging time, I am not alone in my struggle.

I felt a bit more energized as I saw that mom had arranged many things at home to welcome dad. We also planned his birthday celebration for when he would return. While discussing all this, I asked my brother to get some sprouts for dad to eat as he had requested, and I would manage things at home with mom.

Soon, I added a pinch of salt and lemon to the sprouts, just the way dad liked it. Then, mom and I went out to purchase all the necessary items for home care. While shopping, she kept asking for updates about when dad would come home. She suggested buying fruits and healthy vegetables in case he came early. I allayed her, saying, "We can buy those later. I don't know the exact answer, but let's see. Everything is going as per plan."

We came home after a while, feeling a mix of anticipation and hope. We came to know that uncle had also arranged for oxygen cylinders for home use, which was a huge relief. With that sorted, I realized I should visit the hospital now.

Already a bit tired, I reached the hospital and headed straight to the ICU. As I entered, I saw him sitting up, headphones on, listening to music. His oxygen level was steady, hovering between 85 and 90, which was a good sign. Seeing me, he smiled, and I gave him a thumbs-up to show my approval of his oxygen levels. His face brightened with confidence and happiness.

"How is your planning going on at home?" he asked.

"Everything is on track," I replied. "We have an appointment in Delhi tomorrow, and once we meet with the specialist, everything at home is ready for you. So, stay hopeful."

I then asked, "What have you eaten?"

"The doctor advised against sprouts since they require a lot of chewing, so I just had some fruit juices and tofu slices," he said. "It was a good day."

"What were you listening to, dad?" I inquired.

"I was listening to the Lord Hanuman Chalisa," he replied. "It gives me courage."

I showed him the small idol of Lord Hanuman beside his bed, and we both prayed silently, asking for strength to overcome any obstacle. After a moment, I gently pulled at his cheeks and teased, "My cute dad."

He wanted to laugh but hesitated. "I don't want to see myself right now with my growing beard, old and dull face, and you still find me cute."

"Yes, you still are," I insisted.

We shared a laugh, but it made him cough. I quickly steadied him, feeling a mix of joy and concern.

But as he laughed, his throat choked, turning his laughter into a cough. I quickly urged him to relax, and his oxygen levels suddenly plummeted. His eyes, wide red with panic, searched mine for reassurance. I gripped his hand tightly, my legs trembling as I tried to stay calm. "It's okay, dad. Everything's okay. Take deep breaths and relax." I rubbed his shoulder and back, my anxiety rising as I followed up on the monitor.

He trusted me, closed his eyes, and started taking deep breaths. Slowly, his oxygen levels began to improve, and I let out a breath of relief. Dad gripped my hand firmly, his teary, wide eyes filled with unspoken

emotions. This moment, I knew, would stay with me forever. I couldn't forget his eyes, filled with emotions, love, faith, and trust in me. It left a deep imprint on my soul.

He motioned for me to come closer, and with a shaky hand, he gestured as if writing on his palm. "O2?" I asked, confused at first. He repeated the gesture, pointing at me and then slowly spelling out "oxygen" on his palm. This time, his emotions gripped him, rendering it difficult for him to speak.

"YOU ARE MY OXYGEN"

In that quiet exchange, I felt the profound depth of his love and gratitude. Dad couldn't speak, not due to oxygen deprivation, but because overwhelming emotions have left him speechless. Our relationship has always been characterized by sibling-like banter and teasing, and dad seldom openly expressed his affection. Yet now, through his eyes and gestures, he communicates everything he has never vocalized. At that moment, memories flood back—moments lived with him that never hinted at such a heartfelt expression of love, especially not in a situation where he battles for his life daily. I feel helpless, left only to hope and pray. Witnessing this side of him, so rarely revealed, filled me with pride. It felt like a revelation, deepening our bond in unexpected ways.

As I held back my tears, I struggled to keep myself from crying. I hid my face a little, feeling an overwhelming urge to hug my dad tightly and cry my heart out. I could see tears welling up in his eyes, too. After a brief silence, I asked softly, "dad, are you feeling okay now?"

He replied in a shaky voice, engulfed in emotions, "Yes, as long as you are here with me, I am fine."

After a moment of silence, dad shared a dream he had the previous night. In his dream, he saw his beloved God, Lord Hanuman, who assured him he would be relieved from all his pain within the next two days and would return home. A devout follower, my dad believed this dream wholeheartedly. "I trust him now," he said, his voice filled with conviction. "This can't be wrong, as I have truly worshipped him my entire life."

"That's great news!" I responded, trying to match his newfound positivity. "See, even he is with you now, so don't worry, everything will be fine." His face lit up with hope and positivity. When I asked if I should leave, he quickly replied, "No, please stay for a while longer. Sit here and ask the doctor for extra permission until the time I am here in the hospital."

"Yes, I will try. Don't worry," I assured him. We continued our conversation for about thirty minutes. I stood by his side, exchanging words, when the doctor, accompanied by another physician, approached us. Taking my dad's hands in his, the doctor said gently, "Gaur sir, you must have done some great deeds in the past to have a child like her. I observe her every day and how she deals with this situation. I even use her as an example to my colleagues. I watch on the camera how she cares for you and does her best."

Dad, lying down, extended his hand as much as he could and thanked the doctor, showing his agreement. "You're right; there is definitely God's blessing on me," he said sincerely.

The doctor tapped my dad's shoulder proudly and then turned to me, offering the same gesture. "How is your health now?" he asked my dad. "How are you feeling?"

"Everyone here is taking good care of me, and I trust the process and you. I believe I will recover from this," my dad replied.

The doctor encouraged him, saying, "Keep up this spirit, and you will be fine." He then suggested that my dad undergo C-PAP therapy more often, even if he didn't like it, as it was crucial for his recovery. My dad took this advice seriously.

As the doctor turned to leave, dad started sobbing softly. I moved closer, gently pressing his weakened and brittle feet. Through his tears, he uttered words that touched my heart deeply: "You know, this is my real achievement in life—having a dedicated child and a loving family. What more could I ask for?"

I wiped away his tears, feeling a surge of pride and gratitude. "Yes, dad, for me too, this is a proud moment," I replied, my voice quivering with emotion. "Being here for you, spending time with you—it's a privilege and an honor. You've always been my guiding light, my source of strength. And now, being by your side during this challenging time, the love that runs deep within us."

In that moment, amidst the tears and the doubtfulness, there was a profound sense of pride. Despite the hardships we faced and the obstacles we overcame, we stood together, united in love and unwavering support. My dad's words echoed in my mind, reminding me of the precious gift of family, which was our greatest achievement—a legacy that would endure for generations to come.

I was asked to leave the ICU by a nurse, so I assured dad that I would come back. My mom usually visited him during the evening, but I decided to come back with mom in the late evening. After spending some time with him, I left the hospital, feeling a mix of hope and heaviness.

7:00 PM late evening, as I reached the hospital with my mom and aunt, it was already a bit late for visiting time. Mom immediately went inside the ICU while I was waiting outside with family, and after a while, mom came out of the ICU with mixed emotions on her face. Before I could ask anything, she said, "dad is calling you inside. He wants to meet you. It was a short meeting with me."

Feeling a mix of confusion and urgency, I got up and headed into the ICU to meet dad.

I went into the ICU, and as soon as he saw me, he immediately said, "Take care of everyone, especially your mom, as she is sensitive and weak with her emotions. Also, please ask the nurse if she wants to give any medicine to me. I want it to be done in front of you."

I asked the nurse if there were any medicines for the night. She came with a pack of medicines and gave them to dad in front of me. He seemed scared and dependent on me.

At that moment, I hoped he would be home soon. I gave him the prasad from the pooja I performed daily for him every evening since he was hospitalized. He took it with gratitude and asked me to help with his growing beard the next day, as he didn't like keeping a beard. I noted his request and asked him to rest.

He then said, "Please, be here with me tomorrow morning. Ask someone else to go to the doctor's appointment in Delhi." I assured him I would be there and mentioned that my brother was right outside for the whole night. "Don't think you are alone. We are just minutes away, so relax and take proper rest," I said. He again asked the nurse if there was anything left. She laughed with the other nurses and said, "You already took a pack of medicines. Do you still need more?" I joined in the laughter, and he smiled and said good night to everyone.

As I was leaving the hospital with my mom, she shared her conversation with dad. She had asked him to move a little because constant lying down could be problematic for his mobility. He said, "Even when I move, my oxygen levels fluctuate. How can I move and do exercises?" She seemed worried, visibly seeing dad's health deteriorate, but we were still hoping for improvement. Hope was all we had left. I consoled mom, saying that this was a long process and not an overnight journey, but she still seemed worried about his critical condition.

"Mom, these are the only treatments the doctor can give him. What else can we do other than wait? We'll know more from tomorrow's appointment in Delhi. The specialist has researched COVID-19 post-symptoms and is already guiding the doctor here. He's in touch with us," I uphold her.

Soon we arrived home, and a somber atmosphere settled over us all. Mom relayed the same story to the rest of the family, and we ate our meal in quiet solemnity, each of us holding onto hope and saying our prayers for dad's recovery. Later, we all struggled to find sleep, our minds heavy with worry.

A Note from Dad: Strength in Every Word

DAY Fourteen: Facing the Inevitable

Throughout the night, sleep escaped me. My mind raced with worries, and each wave of panic prompted me to pray fervently for my dad's well-being. I eagerly awaited morning, longing to see him again. Thoughts of Dad flooded my mind as I tossed and turned in bed.

I recalled his vibrant life—always living in the moment, easing every situation with humor. He was everyone's go-to person, always ready to lend a helping hand. That's who he was.

Memories flooded back—our playful arguments over trivial things, like him teasing me with my towel. I could still picture his mischievous grin. We'd debate over TV shows; he preferred the news while I wanted music videos. These memories brought both tears and smiles, cherished moments etched in my heart.

In the quiet of the night, I prayed earnestly, "Please, I can't bear to see my dad like this, like a wounded lion lying helplessly in a hospital bed." Memories continued to wash over me, evoking laughter and tears simultaneously. I saw his lively face, now so vulnerable, and my heart ached.

He is the pillar of our family, always strong and dependable. Seeing him weak was almost unbearable. I prayed for strength, for him and for us. I prayed for a miracle, for his recovery.

I remembered how he made every family gathering lively, his laughter filling the room. He taught me to drive a car and ride a bike, comforting me through failures. He wasn't just a father; he is my friend, my mentor, and my hero.

As the night dragged on, I found myself caught in a loop of these memories, unable to break free. The love and admiration I felt for him only grew stronger with each passing thought. I was reminded of his tenacity, his unwavering spirit, and his endless love in different ways.

I managed to sleep for a short while but woke up again at 5:00 AM. The thoughts swirling in my mind made it impossible to rest. I thought about calling my brother, who was at the hospital, but resisted, intimidated it might be too early. My restlessness grew as I worried about dad. Was he able to sleep? It had been a long night. Was he listening to the music he had requested? When he called the nurse for help, did they respond promptly? These questions haunted me.

Unable to find peace, I got out of bed around 5:30 AM and decided to sip some warm water. The cold morning air nipped at my skin as I opened the main door. Dense fog seeped into the room as if it was trying to communicate something. The cool breeze mixed with the fog felt refreshing for a moment. I took deep breaths, trying to calm my racing thoughts. The house was still; everyone was asleep, and the sun had yet to rise.

I returned to bed, phone in hand, contemplating calling my brother. Eventually, I put the phone down, deciding to wait a bit longer. I closed my eyes and prayed for dad's well-being. By 6:15 AM, I couldn't resist any longer. I called my brother, who picked up on the first ring. The sound of ICU vital meters beeped in the background, causing my heart to race.

"What happened?" I asked, my voice trembling.

He tried to sound calm, but I could hear the tension. "Everything is okay, but Mausaji's oxygen levels are dropping. They called me a few minutes ago to bring some medicine."

"How low are the levels?" I pressed, needing to know the exact number.

"Sister, it's low," he replied reluctantly.

"Tell me the exact number," I insisted.

"It's 55-60 and not going up. Everyone is trying their best," he finally admitted.

My heart sank. "What? Is the doctor there?"

"Yes, many nurses are here, coordinating with the doctor over the phone."

"I'm coming," I declared, unable to stay away any longer.

"You can come after some time," he suggested, but I could hear dad's voice faintly in the background, asking if I was on the call.

"Tell her not to go to Delhi for a doctor's appointment today and come here," dad had said.

"I'm not going anywhere. I'll be there soon," I assured him.

I quickly freshened up. By then, my mom and other family members were awake, bombarding me with questions about dad's condition. "Let me go. He's calling for me," I said, trying to remain composed.

"But it's too early. Is something serious?" They asked, concern etched on their faces.

I felt like I was in a daze; my mind focused only on getting to the hospital. "Have patience and don't panic. Everything will be fine. Let me go and see," I affirmed them, though I was barely convincing myself.

As I left, I called my uncle, telling him to come to the hospital because dad wasn't doing well. My second call was to the doctor. "Dad's oxygen is very low," I informed him, my voice shaking.

"We know. We've been monitoring him and have given him injections and drips. We're waiting for his oxygen levels to stabilize. Tests are already underway. We don't have any other choice but to trust the process," he explained.

I hung up, feeling a mix of distress and determination. I had to be strong for dad and my family. With every step toward the hospital, I prayed for strength and for a miracle.

I reached the hospital in a hurry and went straight to the ICU. My heart sank as I saw dad sitting up and sweating, gasping for air. The vital monitor showed his oxygen levels had plummeted to fifty-one despite being on a high oxygen supply, and his blood pressure was dangerously high at 200/115. The machine beeped sharply, echoing my inner panic.

"Dad, try to relax," I said, holding his hand tightly. He was trying his best but struggled with each breath. Seeing him like this was unbearable. I pleaded with him to take deep breaths. He gripped my hand; his body drenched in sweat despite the AC and an extra fan. The cold weather outside seemed irrelevant in this moment of crisis.

Dad leaned back, trying to find some comfort. His oxygen levels crept up to 58, then fifty-nine. He motioned for the fan, needing it on his face. I held it close to him. Frustration overtook him, and he banged his fist on the bed. He was fighting with everything he had, but it didn't seem to be enough.

Feeling helpless, I took out a small idol of Lord Hanuman from my pocket and held it before him. "Dad, pray," I whispered. He touched the idol's feet and began praying. I placed it on the table in front of him so he could keep his eyes on it.

"Are you going to Delhi today?" he asked, his voice weak.

"No, dad. I'm right here with you," I assured him. "I won't go anywhere."

He nodded and then asked about uncle. "Where is he?"

"I called him while leaving the house. He should be here any minute," I replied, trying to sound positive despite my existing condition.

I glanced at the monitor again; his levels were still dangerously low. I sought out the doctors, asking them about his condition. They explained they were monitoring him closely, administering necessary medications, and had already conducted tests. "His oxygen level is critically low, and his CO_2 levels are alarmingly high. We're doing everything we can," one of them said.

They asked me to leave, as they needed space to work. "Please," I begged, "let me stay. I won't disturb you. My presence might help him."

Reluctantly, they agreed. I stood by his side, watching helplessly as they injected him with medications and adjusted his drips. He had become a pin cushion for needles, his body covered in bruises and marks from the constant poking.

"Dad, I'm here," I whispered, holding his hand. I could see the distress in his eyes, mirroring my own. He looked at me with a mixture of hope and desperation, silently begging for relief. I prayed fervently, my heart aching with the sheer powerlessness of the situation.

As I stood there, I was struck by how life had changed so drastically. Dad, once so vibrant and energetic, now lay frail and exposed. Memories of our times together flooded my mind. His laughter, his courage, his zeal to live life each moment – they all seemed so distant now. I couldn't bear to see him like this, reduced to such a frail state.

The morning stretched on, filled with the constant beeping of machines and the hushed whispers of the medical staff. Every second felt like an eternity. I prayed, wishing for a miracle, hoping that dad would pull through. The fright of losing him was a weight on my chest, making it hard to breathe. I held onto his hand, drawing strength from his presence, even in such a dire state.

Dad had always been my anchor, my source of stability. Now, it was my turn to be his. And so, I stayed by his side, praying and hoping, willing him to fight and stay with us.

Dad's fluctuating vital signs were growing increasingly unstable, with each reading more troubling than the one before. The ICU team had gathered around him, urgently administering medications and drawing blood for tests. I stood there, gripped by consternation but clinging to the hope that a miracle would occur and dad would stabilize.

The emergency doctor entered and asked me to leave the room. Other familiar faces, knowing me well by now, echoed the request. I wasn't ready to leave, but the necessity of the situation forced my hand. Tears began to roll down my cheeks. Dad, sensing my reluctance, motioned for me to go and wait outside. His hand, already weak, slipped from mine as I tried to hold on tightly. "I'm fine. You can go. Let them do their work," he managed to say.

Slowly, I backed away to the door, my eyes never leaving dad. From across the room, he raised his thumb, trying to elevate my confidence. His oxygen levels had dropped alarmingly to 45-48, and his heartbeat was dangerously low. Leaving him alone in that room was the hardest thing I'd ever done. Outside, I found my family waiting. My uncle tried to console me as my tears flowed uncontrollably. "Everything will be fine, don't worry," he said, though his own eyes betrayed his concern.

I sat outside the ICU, trying to peek in, but I could see little. After what felt like an eternity, a doctor emerged and asked me to come inside. "He needs to be on a ventilator right now. Please sign the documents and complete the formalities," he said. The shock rendered me unable to think straight. I turned to my uncle, who took charge, agreeing to the ventilator and starting the paperwork.

"This can't be real," I thought, my mind racing. Dad had always frightened this outcome. How must he be feeling right now? My uncle, sensing my turmoil, guided me back into the room. He signed the necessary papers and then asked me to wait inside while everything was being prepared. As we waited, a nurse came in, looked at my uncle, and asked him to step into the ICU. I demanded to know what was happening, but he just said, "Just wait here."

The weight of his words and the unknown gnawed at me. My heart pounded as I tried to make sense of the situation. The uncertainty was unbearable, and the minutes felt like hours. I was on the brink of panic, feeling helpless and desperate for answers.

Moments later, I heard a whisper that made my blood run cold. "His heart has stopped."

"What?" I gasped, looking at my brother's face, which mirrored my shock and terror. We were speechless, caught in a moment of utter disbelief. The world seemed to stand still, every second stretching into an eternity as I tried to process the unthinkable. My mind raced, struggling to comprehend the gravity of the situation. It felt as though the ground had been pulled out from under us, leaving us suspended in a void of unpredictability and dread.

My brother's eyes, wide and filled with anguish, met mine. In that silent exchange, I could see the same questions and doubts swirling in his mind. The room, once familiar and comforting, now seemed foreign and cold, echoing with the weight of our silent despair. Tears welled up in my eyes, blurring my vision as I reached out to hold my brother's hand.

My uncle rushed into the ICU, and soon, I heard the rhythmic, urgent noise of CPR being administered. The sounds of the medical team trying to bring dad back and put him on a ventilator echoed in the hallway; each beat a harrowing reminder of the life-and-death struggle happening just a few feet away.

A surge of anger and despair overwhelmed me, a torrent of emotions I could no longer contain. In a fit of helpless rage, I threw the idol of Lord Hanuman that I had been clutching in my hand. "Why is this happening to me?" I screamed internally. "Why is this happening to my dad? Does God even exist?"

Tears streamed down my face as I grappled with the unfairness of it all. The idol lay broken on the floor, a symbol of my shattered faith. My heart ached with an intensity I had never known, and my mind swirled with questions that had no answers. The pain was unbearable, a deep, searing agony that tore through my soul.

In that moment of utter vulnerability, I felt completely alone despite the presence of my family nearby. The weight of the situation pressed down on me, suffocating and relentless. I sank to my knees, feeling the cold, hard floor beneath me, and sobbed uncontrollably. My body shook with the force of my grief, and I whispered, "Please, let him be okay. Please, let him come back to us."

My brother hugged me tightly, trying to offer comfort. "Believe," he whispered, though his voice wavered with his uneasiness.

Moments later, my uncle emerged from the ICU with a look of calm and peace that contrasted sharply with the chaos inside. He hugged me and said, "I have witnessed a miracle. When I entered the room, he had no heartbeat. But they managed to bring him back with CPR. Have hope and belief. Right now, he is stable and has been put on a ventilator. I saw him come back from nothing. Trust in this moment."

I couldn't stop crying, the emotions flooding over me in waves. The sight of dad's struggle and the fragility of his condition were too much to bear. I left the doctor's room, feeling completely shattered, and sat outside the ICU. Many people there looked at me with understanding and sympathy, sensing the gravity of the situation.

My uncle urged everyone to keep me from going back into the ICU room, knowing that seeing dad on a ventilator would be too traumatic for me. I could only imagine the machines, the tubes, the sterile beeps and clicks that now surrounded my father. I felt utterly helpless, my heart breaking with every passing second.

As I sat there, waiting and praying, I was filled with a profound mix of hope and dread. This was the hardest moment of my life, But I knew I had to stay strong. For dad, for my family, and for myself. We were all in this together, and somehow, we would get through it. But I didn't know how. The hope my uncle had witnessed gave me a flicker of light in the darkness. And for that flicker, I held on with all my might.

My heart was a battlefield of determination and turmoil. I looked around at my family, their faces etched with worry and exhaustion. I wiped my tears, taking deep breaths to steady myself. The rhythmic beeping from the ICU reminded me that Dad was still fighting, and so must I.

During my turmoil, I remembered the strength Dad had always shown, his unwavering resolve in the face of adversity. It was his spirit that I needed to channel now. With each breath, I tried to absorb his courage, to find a way to transform my anguish into grit.

I desperately wanted to see my dad, to hug him, and never let go, but I was paralyzed. I couldn't bear to see him in such a fragile state. Two nurses came out of the ICU with all the medicines and equipment that had been used for Dad. "We don't need this anymore," one of them said. "He's on the ventilator now; he won't need any of this."

A Stranger's Comfort

Each passing moment brought more pain. I sat silently on a chair, sobbing quietly. A gentleman noticed my distress and approached me. "Is he your father inside?" he asked gently.

"Yes," I replied, my voice barely above a whisper.

He inquired about dad's health and what had happened. I gave him a brief description of the events that led us here. He listened attentively, then shared his own story. "I also had my father admitted to this same hospital last year when COVID-19 cases were at their peak. He was badly affected. There was an extreme shortage of oxygen. We weren't even allowed to see him. Every moment was terrifying. We constantly heard negative news, and each time I came to the hospital, I saw bodies being taken away. It was terrifying to think that my father's oxygen could be cut off due to the shortage."

He paused, looking into my eyes with understanding and empathy. "You are lucky you get to see your dad every day, talk to him, and know he is getting the oxygen he needs. My father was on a ventilator for three months. We lost all hope, but he regained his strength and consciousness. Now he is completely fine. So, don't lose hope. Everything will be fine. Trust in that."

I nodded, tears streaming down my face. "What else can we do other than pray and trust?" I said.

His story gave me a small but crucial sense of relief amid the turbulence. I thanked him for checking on me and for sharing his experience. His words were a lifeline in my sea of despair, a reminder that miracles could happen, even in the darkest of times.

As I sat there, trying to absorb the stranger's words of hope, I felt a shift within me. Despite the pain and fear, I clung to the possibility of a miracle, just as he had. This stranger's kindness and shared experience had given me a glimmer of hope, and for that, I was profoundly grateful.

My family members urged me to come inside the waiting room, but I chose to stay outside the ICU. Each call from the doctors felt like a death knell. I was praying fervently to the cosmos, to God, to any higher power that might listen. How could I bear to see my dad like this, so helpless? He had always been my biggest strength, and now he is losing his strength. My silent prayers were filled with desperation—please help my dad endure this pain and heal him.

My cousin held my hand and gently led me to the waiting room, offering me water. My hands were trembling as I sipped, my thoughts scattered, and my heart heavy. I was still sobbing quietly when a nurse came in and announced my dad's name, asking for a family member to fetch some medicinal liquid. My cousin hurried to comply, leaving me with my thoughts and the concerned glances of other people in the room. They wanted to say something, to comfort me, but perhaps they held back, sensing my fragile state.

After a few minutes, I couldn't bear sitting still any longer. I got up and moved back to the ICU, pacing restlessly outside the doors. I saw my brother inside, looking at my dad's bed with a stunned expression. I could only see from afar, imagining countless scenarios, each one more dreadful than the previous. Minutes later, my brother came out, his face masked but his eyes wet with tears. He approached me and hugged me tightly, saying nothing.

"What happened? What happened?" I asked frantically, but he remained silent.

Then I saw my uncle coming out of the ICU, signing some documents. A wave of dread enveloped me. I needed someone to tell me what was going on. My uncle walked toward me, and without any preamble, he said, "dad is no longer with us."

"What? What? What does this even mean?" My ears felt numb, and I could only hear my heartbeats thudding in my chest. Everything else around me became a blur, the sounds fading away. I heard the words, but how could I believe them?

My world shattered in an instant. The words were simple, but the reality was unbearable. I felt an overwhelming sense of disbelief and anguish. How could my dad be gone? The pain was too immense to process, the loss too great to comprehend. My legs gave way, and I sank to the floor, sobbing uncontrollably. My brother and uncle tried to console me, but their words were just echoes in the void that had opened inside me.

I sat there on the cold hospital floor, my mind reeling. The man who had always been my pillar of strength was gone. The room around me was filled with people, but I felt utterly alone. At that moment, I was lost in a sea of grief and despair. Every memory of him flooded my mind—his laughter, his wisdom, his unconditional love. It was as if the very foundation of my life had crumbled beneath me.

The reality of my dad's absence slowly started to sink in. I realized that I would never hear his voice again, never feel his backing presence. My heart ached with an emptiness that words could never describe. As I sat there, surrounded by my grieving family, I understood that life would never be the same. The man who had given me so much love and guidance was gone, leaving behind a void that nothing could ever fill.

Stone-cold ICU

My uncle came closer, and soon, my other cousins arrived at the hospital. Soon, my thoughts turned to my mom, who was at home waiting for dad. She was preparing for his return, but she never imagined it would be like this. How would I tell her that he would come home not as her husband, but as a lifeless body? I was terrified at the thought.

My uncle told me to go inside and see dad one last time. Was this the last time I would see him? As I sat on the floor, numb with grief, my uncle and brother helped me to my feet and led me to the ICU. There, behind a curtain, lay my dad. When the curtain was pulled back, I saw him lying without the oxygen mask that had become a permanent fixture on his face. His head was tilted to the side, and there was an immense peace on his face as if he were in a deep sleep, serene sleep. I hadn't seen him without an oxygen mask in many days. How could he be sleeping so peacefully without it?

Thoughts raced through my mind. I wanted him to wake up, to speak to me, to ask about his condition. I believed I was his oxygen, and that he would be fine when I was around. Why did I leave when the doctor asked me to? I should have stayed with him; maybe then he would still be alive. He had given me a thumbs-up, assuring me he was fine—what had happened in those twenty minutes? Everything had changed.

I held my dad's hand, which felt loose and lifeless but still warm and soft. He had fought so hard for his life. His beard, which he had asked me to shave just yesterday, was still there. As I held his hand, I noticed a blue patch where the cannula had been. I wondered if there was still any hope that, somehow, he could come back to us. The life we had just fourteen days ago—singing songs, laughing, talking—would that never come again? The hospital staff referred to him as a "dead body." Was he no longer my dad? What had changed in him so drastically that he no longer responded? The contrast between those vibrant recollections and the stark reality before me was too much to bear.

I wanted to tell him so much: how much I loved him, admired him, and all the emotions I had never shared. But how could I now? Would he hear me? I started talking to his soul, believing he must still be around, trying to communicate. I asked him why he left. How would I tell mom, who was waiting at home, that he would never come back? Would she be able to handle it? He always said she had a weak heart. How could I tell her that he was gone forever?

As I was asked to leave the ICU, a realization dawned on me. If he was not there, it was his choice. He chose to go because my father would never give up on anything—that's how he is. He must have chosen to leave this cruel world. He was a tiger who always gave hope to everyone he met; he never lost hope for himself. He didn't want to suffer anymore and chose to free himself from everything.

This was my father's final act of strength. Even in his last moments, he was in control. As I walked away from the ICU, I understood that he had found his peace.

As we left the hospital, I was gripped by a new challenge. Telling my mom about dad's passing felt like the hardest task of all. The car ride home was heavy with grief. We were four people, each lost in their sorrow, tears silently streaming down our faces. The car was filled with an awkward silence, punctuated only by the occasional sob. The suddenness of the news had hit us all hard.

When we arrived home, I hesitated at the door, hearing loud cries from inside. My mom, my aunt, and other family members were wailing, their heartbreak echoing through the walls. People were already gathering outside, drawn by the tragedy that had befallen us. My immediate reaction was to rush to my mom and hug her tightly.

As soon as she saw me, her cries grew louder. She clung to me, her pain pouring out in words, "You showed so much courage, prayed, did everything you could. You were dedicated to him these last 14 days, but he still chose to go. Why?" Her words broke me. I held her, both of us crying uncontrollably, surrounded by the sounds of mourning. Others tried to console us, but the depth of our pain was beyond their reach.

I knew I had to gather myself. My mom needed me to be strong. I let her go to be with other family members, taking a deep breath to steady myself. Some things needed to be arranged at home, and I had to take charge. As I began to organize, my mind drifted back to the day dad left for the hospital.

It was his birthday. He had walked out of the house looking so well, combing his hair and putting on his favorite perfume. It felt so casual, like he would be back in no time. Who could have imagined he would return this way? In the hospital, I had promised him a grand birthday celebration when he got better. But life had other plans. Everything seemed like a cruel game, controlled by a higher power, with our lives written in chapters beyond our control.

As dad's body arrived home, the reality of the situation became even more stark. My heart ached, remembering how he had left us, walking confidently, unaware that he would never return alive. Now, here he was, not as the strong man we knew but as a lifeless form.

I felt the weight of this moment, of my responsibilities, and the grief that was now a permanent part of us. Dad's departure had left a void that could never be filled. My mom's pain was unbearable to witness, but I had to be her strength now. I had to be strong for her, for my family, and myself.

The grief in our home was concrete, a heavy fog that hung over every room. My mother's pain was beyond words, a deep well of sorrow that seemed bottomless. She had been unwell even before this, and now her health was a significant concern for all of us. The rituals were performed, each one a step closer to saying the final goodbye to my father. The family, steeped in immense grief, gathered to support each other through this unimaginable loss.

The Final Farewell

As the time came to say the final farewell, I sat beside my father. His lifeless form lay there, but in my heart, he was still very much alive. "Dad," I began, my voice trembling but determined, "you have always been my biggest inspiration, my teacher, my mentor. I promise you that you will live through me, as I am your oxygen now. I have learned so much from you, especially in these last 14 days. Despite the situation, we shared a bond that I will cherish forever. I have seen your courage, and I pray to God that I can be even ten percent of who you were. I promise to become more like you with each passing day of my life."

Tears streamed down my face as I continued, my words a solemn vow. "The time we spent together will be treasured forever. You were so strong, so full of life. You respected each moment of your existence and always helped anyone who came to you without a second thought. You were free from greed and jealousy, sharing only love with everyone. You found joy in others' achievements and happiness in the smallest of things. You lived life on your terms."

"I promise to keep your legacy within me. I will strive to make you proud, to become a good human being, and to take care of our family. Please promise me that you will always guide me in life and always bless me from up there. I would love to be shielded by your aura, your positivity, and your love. I know you are listening, dad. Keep shining in the sky, showering your positivity. Be at peace, in a better place."

As I let go of his hand for the last time, my heart felt both heavy and light. Heavy with the grief of his loss but light with the hope that he was now free from pain and suffering. I stood up, feeling a profound sense of responsibility and a renewed determination to honor his memory. My family and I would carry forward his legacy of love, strength, and integrity.

At that moment, as I looked up at the sky, I felt a strange sense of peace. I knew he was up there, watching over us, guiding us with his eternal love. This was not the end but a new beginning, a journey to live in a way that would make him proud. With that thought, I embraced the path ahead, carrying my father's spirit within me, ready to face the world with the courage and love he had always shown.

Lord Krishna says -

न जायते म्रियते वा कदाचि
नायं भूत्वा भवति वा न भूय: |
अजो नित्य: शाश्वतोऽयं पुराणो
न हन्यते हन्यमाने शरीरे ||

The soul is neither born nor does it ever die; nor, having once existed, does it ever cease to be. The soul is without birth, eternal, immortal, and ageless. It is not destroyed when the body is destroyed – Bhagwat Gita chapter 2, verse 20.

Lord Hanuman: Dad's Devotion During All 14 Days in the ICU

Acknowledgements

Special thanks to all those who have been there for me during my difficult times. Your unwavering support has been my greatest strength.

Neeraj Gaur (mom)

Kapeesh Gaur (Uncle)

Archana Gaur (Aunt)

Mayank Gaur (Brother)

Hina Gaur (Sister)

Puneet Mandela (Aunt)

Manit Mandela (Brother)

And all the family and friends who were not physically present still offered constant support and prayers through communication.

For your valuable feedback email us–
daddysoxygen@gmail.com

9 7 9 8 8 9 4 9 8 4 6 0 5